Wake-Up Call:

A Psychic's Guide
to a Better Life

Live
Laugh
Love

Kim

Wake-Up Call:

A Psychic's Guide
to a Better Life

Kim Sartor
with Christine Cowley

Wake-Up Call: A Psychic's Guide to A Better Life

Kim Sartor in collaboration with Christine Cowley, 2009

Book and Cover design:
Annette Rolland, www.arolland.com

Pre-production:
LifeGems Personal Histories, www.lifegemsbio.com

Front cover image:
Robin photograph by Thomas Crean via ShutterPoint

Back cover image:
Robin photograph by Trev Gainey@hazysunimages.com

Cover image:
Tree photograph by Annette Rolland

Printed in Canada by:
Kempenfelt Graphics Group Inc., www.kggdigital.com

Published by:
Kim Sartor, 2009

ISBN 978-0-557-22363-3

Acknowledgments

I would like to thank the following people for helping
to make this book a reality.

Christine Cowley, for writing it.

Barbara Weider, for the time she spent editing the first manuscript and
for the benefit of her wisdom, which I feel privileged to have received.

Catarina Flack, for being there to help when I needed her.

My customers, for being so loyal.

My husband, for being so patient.

My son, for teaching me something new every day.

My parents, for always believing in me and truly being the
best parents anyone could have.

My sisters, Jackie and Nicole, for never giving up on this dream
to help people.

Chris King, for helping us see the light at the end of the tunnel.

Helen Stone, for providing psychic guidance.

Dorothy Garland, for creating Di-Cerot, the blocks I use
for doing readings.

Kate Eichenberger, for her help, support and encouragement.

Victoria Hendry, for her help, enthusiasm and friendship.

Tom and Bessie Tesseris, for introducing me to life's
true values, in Greece.

Jayne Vaughan, for her strong influence in my life; her example inspires
all women to be as dynamic as they want to be.

Debbie Glover, for showing me that anyone can do what they
put their mind to.

Dr. Jon Barrett and Sue Seymour of Sunnybrook Health Sciences
Centre for their professionalism.

Contents

Introduction

Do not speak in the hearing of a fool
For he will despise the wisdom of your words
. . . Apply your heart to discipline
And your ears to words of knowledge.

Proverbs 23: 9, 12[1]

The single most commonly asked question when people first learn what I do for a living is, "When did you first realize you were psychic?" After doing readings for ten years, I can honestly say there was no single defining moment when I saw my abilities as something extraordinary. A growing understanding of my own capacity to identify the problems plaguing people's lives and to see a clear path through these obstacles made itself known to me at a very early age. I could not have understood as a child the things I understand about people today. But my perception of the emotions, motivations, challenges and strengths of my clients, even at first meeting, has allowed me to help so many people to better understand themselves and to address their lives with authenticity and clarity of purpose far beyond the narrow vision they accepted as the only possible reality.

As a psychic, I have concluded that there are five core issues that affect people in nearly all aspects of their lives—these are: trust, power, natural ability, forgiveness and the consequences of choices. In the following chapters, I will discuss each of these issues as well as the steps you can employ when meeting challenges in all areas of your life that will help increase your personal power. I will provide practical advice based on many years of observation and experience to help focus on creating achievable goals, recognizing natural strengths and weaknesses, and setting boundaries to improve your personal and professional relationships. With respect to career

---

1 All Bible quotations are from the New American Standard Bible.

decisions, I will show how matching your ability with your career choices can help ensure success.

Many astute business people find themselves at a loss in the realm of romance; in chapter four, I reveal some of the most common perils of finding and maintaining healthy relationships, ways to avoid those perils, and remedies to help repair damaged, but important, relationships. The speed at which modern life progresses can overwhelm even the most resilient personality. Some people turn to drugs and alcohol as a means to temporarily deal with stress, only to find they are mired in addiction; or worse, they fail to recognize their problem. Chapter five offers advice and real-life examples that may surprise or shock you: hidden addictions may be the root of your problems. The everyday dramas surrounding money and our relationship with it can be a source of joy or anxiety, engendering generosity and goodwill in one sibling while invoking avarice and rage in another. Our relationship to money and its hold on man since the dawn of civilization is discussed in chapter six. Trust, loyalty, respect and compassion are cornerstones of humanity, defining our place at the top of the food chain. However, in this world of illusory success, these ideals increasingly lose meaning. In chapter seven, the impact of deception and personal secrets on the global community reveals a shocking truth: it is not only in the political arena that secrets and lies undermine the foundation upon which civilizations are built. In chapter eight, you are invited to reclaim their power, regain a sense of direction and commitment, and get behind the wheel that is driving their lives. Finally, I will provide simple, practical exercises to help move you along the path of renewed vitality in all areas of your life. Simple, yes, but don't let that fool you. There is so much joy to be reclaimed from the simplest acts of daily life when undertaken with a new attitude.

In my examples, I refer to my clients by first name; though the people are real, their names have been changed for privacy. These examples are shared for the purpose of showing you that there are other ways to view a situation or circumstance in which you feel powerless, confused, or simply faced with too many potential choices. By providing you with real-life examples of other people's challenges, choices and outcomes, this book offers opportunities for insight into your own situation so that you might discern solutions or possibilities previously hidden from view.

I want to clarify that I am not a doctor and I have no formal psychological training. I am not a saint, and I do not preach from a place of moral superiority. I can only speak from my experience as a psychic, pooled from observations during 10 years of readings and my ability to see auras for 25 years and connect with people's energy. My only purpose is to use this experience, knowledge and intuition to help those people who are ready and willing to improve their lives.

My own path to sharing what I have learned has been a very long one, full of unforeseen twists and turns—yes, even a psychic gets surprises! It is an old but true adage that we can learn more from our failures than from our successes. I had dreamt about writing a book for years. After years of gathering information, studying correlations and recording my observations, I sought the help I needed to put the book together. But numerous setbacks forced me to question my ambition to put these lessons into print. I felt crushed. Did this dream of mine really have a greater purpose or was I simply drawn to writing a book for my own satisfaction? I had to search deep within myself to examine my true motivation and to confirm that my ambition to make this information available was genuine and not ego-driven. I reaffirmed to a Higher Power that my desire and purpose is to use my psychic gift to help others, but not only those individuals whom I could reach personally. Eventually, I understood unequivocally that I was called to share these insights with as many people as I could possibly reach, whoever they are, wherever they live and whatever their present life circumstances. How did I come to this understanding? A little bird told me.

At about the time of my deepest questioning over my mission to share these lessons, a robin took up residence in the tree outside my bedroom window. To announce his arrival, Robin flew into my bedroom window early that first morning, hitting the pane of glass with a loud thud. I was startled awake and ran to the window. Again, Robin hit the pane so hard that I jumped back.

This was the beginning of a campaign. Robin continued to wake me every morning, flying into my bedroom window and hitting the pane of glass. This was no ordinary case of a bird not being able to distinguish the glass window pane. I watched amazed as Robin launched itself from the pine tree in front of the window and hit the glass repeatedly at about ten second intervals. I don't mean it did it once or twice and went away—this went on over and over again for hours at a time, usually in the wee hours of the morning. Sleep? Impossible! It became unnerving to the point of torture!

I tried every suggestion from friends and even strangers on the internet to discourage the bird from its strange behavior. I hung a birdhouse outside to lure the robin away from the window. When I learned robins will attack their reflections to defend their territory, I hung towels outside to cover the window, but the robin persisted, just knocking the towel down. I then tried the suggestion of hanging pieces of ribbon about a ½-inch apart in front of the window. After getting his legs and wings tangled in the ribbon and then getting himself free, the robin continued on his mission of attack. Window decals, flashing lights, a toy snake and stuffed toys suggested by the wildlife center did not change this bird's behavior. Even standing outside the window right in front of him was no deterrent.

I began to sleep with the video camera next to me to capture the robin on tape in an effort to recognize a pattern or hopefully scare him away. I began to wonder whether the robin was some sort of messenger, pushing me to continue to work on my book, in spite of the earlier disappointments. The timing was right, but perhaps my frustration was pushing the reality of the book further away. In chapter three, I share how the dream did in fact come about and the important lesson it taught me about living in sync: moving with the flow of energy instead of pushing against it.

Ultimately, the robin's appearance at my window came down to one simple lesson: wake up! The phrase had been hammering in my head over and over, just like the robin hammering at my bedroom window. It was time to share all the truths I have learned through the readings I have done; it was time to shake up those who are sleep-walking through their lives, continually making poor choices out of foolishness, carelessness or just sheer laziness. When I embraced this idea, suddenly things began to fall into place.

Slowly the book began to unfold. The numerous wake-up calls that my clients had experienced and acted upon—or failed to act upon—laid the foundation for lessons that I could share with others who are willing improve their lives and the lives of others. Those others may be friends, family or even strangers; so much is to be gained from random acts of kindness. This is a lesson shared in the final chapter of this book, which deals with lessons surrounding money and our relationship to it.

Just as my clients are individuals who react in their own way to life's opportunities and challenges, as you read this book you will bring to it your unique perspective and style. Some readers like to sample books, reading various parts or chapters dealing with subject matter that is of particular interest to them. This book is a little different, however, than a traditional how-to book. The information shared in each chapter builds sequentially on lessons and insights shared in previous pages.

One

Auras, Tarot and Guardian Angels

Do not neglect to show hospitality to strangers, for by this
some have entertained angels without knowing it.

Hebrews 13:2

As a child I often felt uneasiness over my ability to *see* and
know very personal and private details of people's lives, even
upon first meeting them. Though I could not understand why,
I knew I had an unusual perception which revealed people's
emotions, their motivations, challenges, and in particular, their
physical state of health. This perception eventually manifested
as colored light, something I now know to be the aura: the
energy or electromagnetic field surrounding the human body.
Everyone has an aura, though in people with serious emotional
or psychological issues, energy may be blocked resulting in
gaps in the electromagnetic field emitted by their bodies. I will

discuss these energy blockages and how to deal with them in chapter two.

At first I only did readings for family and friends. Once I built up my confidence, I began doing readings for other people who had heard about me and eventually opened up my practice to the general public. I wasn't nervous about my ability to give accurate readings, but I still had reservations about what I might see in the readings and how much responsibility I was assuming. Would I see disasters and tragedies? If I did, what was my responsibility to my client? How much should I tell? Would a negative energy be able leave the aura of a client and cling to mine? As I gained confidence, I found my own comfort zone, learning how much to tell and how much to leave out.

When I began to open up my practice to strangers, I found odd things started to happen. Up to that point, I had always known something about the subject of the reading—they were friends and family and it was natural to think that having some knowledge of their circumstances would influence some of what I saw and read. With the general public, however, the messages that came through could not have been from prior knowledge. One client after another stared at me in dismay as I spoke of their lives, loved ones or situation with surprising accuracy. The more I used my natural abilities, the better I was able to *listen* and attune my inner ear to the messages being given. Since starting readings at the age of 33, my psychic abilities have evolved to a much higher level. I want to reiterate that I am not a doctor or a psychologist. The proven accuracy of what I have seen and read for clients over and over is all the confirmation I need to know that my life's purpose is to use my gifts to help people avoid mistakes or to repair the damage they have done to their lives and/or the lives of others.

Tarot Truths and Revelations

The tools I use for my readings are the Di-Cerot Tarot Blocks, psychometry, auras and communication with spirit guides. Though I can see guardian angels, I am unable to communicate directly with them as they exist in a higher realm than the one inhabited by humans and spirit guides. This is covered in greater detail later in this chapter.

For the purpose of clarification, when I make reference to images of the tarot, the interpretations may not be the norm; however, the images described can generally be applied to the traditional tarot deck unless it is specific to a block placement, such as a split path. I have not received any formal training in reading the tarot, and I have a lot of my own psychic feelings that many not conform to other teachings or traditional interpretations.

Just as a traditional set of tarot cards is wrapped in a silk cloth when not in use, my set of Di-Cerot blocks is kept in a silk bag. The set of 13 wooden blocks bears illustrations of the 78 images of the traditional tarot. When a reading begins, I ask the subject to hold the silk bag containing all the blocks, shake them and then cast them on the table in front of me. How the blocks are placed has significance: which blocks are touching, where they land and especially if the blocks are on top of each other. I only read what faces me, reading the blocks as they have been presented. Any part of a block that is not visible doesn't enter into the reading.

Typically, a reading consists of three segments:

- The Past: Begins anywhere from last month to as far back as birth.
- The Present: This encompasses now to six months from now.
- The Future: This is a period of six months to a year. On occasion, I can see further ahead than a year, but only in rare cases.

While I am conducting a reading, I always hold onto something that belongs to the subject. I was fortunate that when I first began readings my psychic abilities were recognized by two gifted psychics who became my mentors. With their help, I was able to hone my psychometric ability; this is the ability to feel vibrations by holding someone's belongings, such as a watch or ring, or even a cell phone, in my hands. In this way, I am able to connect directly to that person's energy. The energy I perceive from objects presents itself as a sort of heat, tingling or vibration in my hands. It is this vibration that conveys the *knowing* I perceive about the person. This knowing is difficult to explain, but the easiest description is to say that it is like walking a mile in their shoes. I share the subject's energy: see, feel and understand things about them in ways that can provide unique insights into their lives. By sharing these insights with them, I can help them make more informed choices that will lead to a more beneficial outcome.

One of the first experiences that showed me this was my role was when I did a reading for an older European gentleman. He had a strong accent, so there was something of a communication barrier, and standing in the doorway he struggled to tell me what he had come to ask me about. I indicated that he should sit down.

The moment he sat down, the most extraordinary thing happened: a young woman with blonde hair and wings suddenly appeared, hovering just over his head. I was so overcome with emotion I started to cry. In that moment, I became convinced that angels really do exist—I could see one for myself. When I started to cry, the man looked puzzled. Then I described to him what I had just seen. A look of dismay and sadness passed over his face, and he began to tell me his story.

His daughter had recently been killed in a car accident; he was overwhelmed with grief and could not bear the thought of never seeing her again. He felt her presence near to him, and yet he was powerless to reach out and draw her back into the land of the living. He told me that the wound seemed impossible to heal if he could not be with her. I told him that part of the reason I was crying was that I knew he was contemplating joining his daughter in death. I told him he must not do this and that his daughter was staying by his side to make sure he stayed in this life, on the earth, until it was his time to pass. I knew it was correct to tell him that she would be with him always. From that point on, I started to collect angel images of all kinds; they surround me to serve as a constant reminder of that glorious moment.

PERCEPTION AND MEANING OF AURA CHARACTERISTICS

Following the reading where I saw the man's daughter/angel, I gained the confidence and understanding that my gift was to be shared. I began seeing auras—the energy field which manifests as colored light surrounding the bodies of living organisms: humans, animals and plants. This soft emanation of light can project anywhere from two to 24 inches from the body. The colors I see reveal everything from hidden surgery scars to deep and private emotional ones. As I began to perceive auras, I was able to identify characteristics of certain illnesses or disturbances within the physical body.

Faced with this responsibility, I am presented with the often difficult moral issue of whether or not to tell a client of potential or present health problems I perceive. I am not a doctor, nor can I diagnose disease. But I believe that by telling people what I see, something most people cannot see, I can lead them to seek appropriate help or to change negative behavior before a situation becomes critical or even irreversible. Observing and decoding key information represented by aura characteristics is an important part of my role. Much of the information provided in this book deals with aura characteristics, what they mean and how individuals can alter their emotional and mental states in order to improve the quality of energy their bodies transmit.

Since nearly two-thirds of the human body is water, it is not surprising that we are tremendous conductors of energy. The energy held and transmitted by our bodies tells our stories. It tells whether we are creative, angry, ready to move forward, in healing mode, or whether we are here to help other people to heal; it provides clues to issues that must be dealt with before we can move on to other things or find our life's work. When I look at someone, I see their energy body surrounding them which manifests in one or several colors and may contain many variants. These variants may appear to me as spots or larger areas of different colors: orange, red, green, violet; there may be black spots or grey areas; hopefully, there are no trailing wisps of grey. I will explain about the grey wisps in chapter five.

Here is an exercise that can help you perceive a person's aura. Have a friend sit with their back against a white wall. Looking toward the top of the head relax your eyes as if you were looking at something beyond the person. You should feel your vision becoming slightly blurred. Keep looking above your friend's head; soon you should start to see a haze start to take shape. At first, it may just appear as a shadow, but if you stay focused on the shadow, it will start to take on subtle characteristics of color and shape. Don't expect to see vibrant colors; auras are not like illustrations of halos or rainbows, but rather more along the lines of the Northern Lights. The more you practice this exercise, the more you can improve your ability to perceive colors and even more subtle characteristics, such as blockages, dullness or retraction of auras.

You don't need a psychic to identify or interpret auras; there are many tools on the market today that reveal aura color. A special photographic process captures and saves an auric image. This method has been refined to a highly scientific degree; studies on the perception and significance of auras continue. Just as with many previously unexplained or unproven claims or beliefs regarding the existence of things beyond normal human perception, the existence of auras will become accepted as a common fact one day.

Now that you have seen your friend's aura, you may be intrigued to know what the colors mean. Though psychics and others who see and read auras may have their own interpretations, my knowledge of what aura characteristics tell me about a person's circumstances, physical condition or personality traits are based on the many readings I have conducted over the years, with proof often following in a later outcome—whether or not my advice to the individual was taken to heart.

Some of the most common colors visible in the aura are: white, violet, gold, olive green/mustard yellow, blue, green, orange and red; pink is rarely seen, but I have included it here for those who may see it, as I have done.

Here are some of the most common characteristics of the aura colors:

White denotes purity. White auras usually surround people who work with the elderly, children and animals. People with white auras seem to be easily taken advantage of due to their giving, trusting natures. Although they have a need and desire to help others, they are often unable to help themselves, especially when they need it the most. These people might be represented as the archetypal wounded healer depicted in the tarot card of The Hierophant or as The High Priestess, both of which represent aspects of spiritual and emotional enlightenment.

Violet denotes loyalty and trustworthiness. Violet people are in touch with their higher selves. They usually concern themselves with spiritual matters. I have found them to be very genuine people.

Gold is connected to a higher power. Gold is an indication of old souls, prophets, leaders and healers. In images of Catholic saints or religious icons, the subject is usually surrounded by a gold or white halo; this is a depiction of the early understanding of auras. Nurses, doctors, social workers and some teachers often demonstrate gold auras, an indication of their vocation to the fields of healing or self-knowledge. When I did a reading for a dog groomer, I saw her hands surrounded by a golden glow. From this, I knew that she had the natural ability to work soothingly with my skittish dog (rescued after being abandoned)—and she has for years, without incident.

Olive Green/**Mustard Yellow** suggests deceit or duplicity. When I see this color in a person's aura I know I am in the presence of an extremely untrustworthy person or a compulsive liar. Their morality train is off the rails; they have lost the ability or desire to discern that their destructive habits, actions or decisions are hurtful to others. Often they experience a boomerang effect and find their negative output lands back in their own lives. This is what has commonly come to be called "creating bad karma." The principle of karma is a bit more complex than that, but you get the idea. If there are only areas around the body which indicate the presence of this color, the client may be suffering from self-deception.

Grey is often accompanied or followed by the olive green/ mustard yellow. Grey is a seriously scary aura color. When I see these grey wisps clinging to a person's aura, I know that I am in the presence of someone who has opened their energetic field to extremely negative vibrations or entities. Drug addicts bear the burden of these spooky, grey wisps. These are entities that are able to attach themselves to the aura of a drug user while the user is under the influence of narcotics; the human addict's spiritual essence has been attacked and is literally being sucked dry by the greys. In chapter five, I discuss the greys and the extremely serious hazards to which so-called "recreational" drug users expose themselves when they get high.

Blue is usually mixed with white and denotes a practical, "feet on the floor" attitude. Blue is seen in the auras of stable, grounded people; what I call the earthbound realists of the planet. My sister Nicole, an engineer, has some blue at the top of her aura. Accompanying Nicole to her office party one year at the plant where she worked was like being at a blue aura convention—a hall filled with engineers, architects, planners, contractors and construction workers: a group of earthbound realists, to be sure.

Green indicates healing. When I see a lot of green around a person, no matter how sick they are or have been, it's a good thing because it tells me that they are in healing mode. This can be physical or emotional healing. You can actually help your body or your emotions to heal by visualizing yourself with emerald green light around you. Keep thinking about emerald green and rely on the vast power of your mind to start or speed up the healing process.

Orange indicates very creative or social people. I usually perceive orange auras around writers, musicians, decorators, entertainers, artists, dancers and even inspirational speakers. If I see a lot of orange in a person's aura, it can indicate that they are craving more self-expression. They may need to find ways to express themselves or work through some emotions through writing or music.

Red is the least straightforward of all the aura colors, since it can manifest a wide variety of characteristics that indicate various interpretations. Sometimes I will see the color red layered over auras. This tells me of temporary emotional states; if I see dark red over the whole aura, it tells me that the individual harbors a great deal of anger and/or resentment: hence the expression, "seeing red." Conversely, a beautiful bright red can indicate that the subject is in love. Red layers over individual parts of the body can signify anything from an unhealthy inflammation to sexual resentment or interference. Red is often indicative of a moody or distressed person. I associate a very deep black-red with evil, a precursor of the grey wisps.

Pink is rarely seen in an aura, however, I have observed it and identify it as an indication of innocence, peace and a non-judgmental view of the world. If I see pink or white on someone's shoulder, it means either that a baby is coming or there has been a recent miscarriage. In the case of a miscarriage, it seems the innocent soul stays for awhile to help guide and comfort the parent through the grief of their loss.

Besides variations in color, an aura can take on many other characteristics. For instance, its shape and size can vary; if it clings closely to the body it can mean there are serious health and/or emotional issues; a person who consumes a diet high in chemical additives often exhibits a pulsating aura, as if their body is jolting or having spasms. I see this as an indication that their bodies are constantly fighting things like aspartame and other unhealthy additives.

Auras that are located more to the left side of the body indicate a person who is predominantly a left-brain thinker: these people are practical, logical and pragmatic; for instance, engineers; an aura located more on the right side of the body, indicates a right-brain thinker: artists, musicians, writers and others whose predominant characteristics are of a creative nature.

An aura that seems to be moving in all directions indicates a very imbalanced state of mind. These people are often helped by the use of quartz crystals to balance their confusion and absorb negativity.

In most of the people I see, the emanation of the aura begins at the feet, connecting to the ground but flowing upward and/or outward. Auras that don't touch the ground indicate people who are less attached to all the things and people of this world. I refer to these people as floaters: they are usually creative but often flighty and unsettled, flitting from one relationship or project to another, seldom committing wholeheartedly to anything; they often fail to complete undertakings. Floaters prefer to live without a plan, letting the winds of the world carry them along on its travels. Sometimes a person who experiences a sudden flood of creativity will feel ungrounded, making decisions around work difficult and actually impeding their ability to produce tangible results. When this happens, their ungrounded aura literally needs to be pinned to the earth. When someone tells me they suddenly feel ungrounded and crave stability and clarity of mind, I recommend they carry a piece of hematite for its magnetic properties. Throughout this book, you will learn various methods of healing or clearing unwanted characteristics from your aura.

Auras are in a constant state of movement and color change. I think of auras as a visual indicator of a person's energy, which is subject to all the influences of circumstance, negative/positive attitudes and physical highs and lows. A healthy aura is infused with white or pastel colors and is fully translucent. When I see a more luminous aura, I find the individual to be relaxed, content and generous. In contrast, darkness and density are indicative of negative emotions such as anger, resentment and fear. Healthy energy flows freely around the entire body without any gaps or blockages. Gaps, pockets or holes can appear in an aura as dark spots or pockets of dead energy (no energy); these indicate places where the energy flow has been interrupted, sometimes temporarily, by illness or emotional/mental negativity. When I see pockets or holes, it quite often relates to significant physical problems; for instance, a person with hearing problems will demonstrate an aura that shows gaps or holes around the ears.

The aura can expand and retract; this is generally in response to emotions and mental states; for example: if your sense of safety is compromised your aura will retract, almost as if trying to shelter and protect you. I am sure that you have felt fear at some point, perhaps walking alone late at night. If you tuned in to how you were feeling at the time, you might recognize that you actually tried to become less visible until you felt safe again. Your aura probably responded by making itself as invisible or as dark as possible.

I see the aura's ability to instantly change or mutate during some of my readings. My readings are not sugar-coated, and they are often hard for the subject to swallow. I recall a reading I gave for a woman whose son was getting involved with drugs; when I told her what I was seeing, she denied any possibility that it was true. As the reading progressed, her anger became very apparent by changes in her aura. I watched as her aura first retracted, then glowed dark red and began to pulsate like a coiled snake ready to strike. Her aura told me loud and clear that she did not like what she was hearing. A footnote to this example is that I learned some months later that the woman discovered that I was correct; still, she made excuses for her son's behavior. Knowledge does not always illuminate, especially in the case of determined denial.

Never underestimate the power of denial.

Anger and fear are not the only reason for an aura to retract. Emotional pain, such as grief over the death of a loved one, or someone who is suffering in an abusive relationship can cause an aura to retract. This type of retraction could be likened to wrapping a protective quilt around the person. While this type of protection might be acceptable or even beneficial for short periods of time, maintaining a retracted aura for any extended length of time is not healthy. A retracted aura repels others, making it almost impossible for anyone to come into your life, perhaps at a time when you most need the comfort, caring and company of others. You can probably envision this by making a comparison with the crossed swords in the tarot deck. When the knight with two crossed swords appears, there is no energy coming in or going out—it's a stalemate. This best describes the state of the person who feels so anguished they have pulled their aura tightly in around them; they think that they will never let it expand again! This is not a good state of mind and will only lead to further emotional and possibly physical harm.

My sister Jackie is also a psychic. Jackie's ability to zone into the energy she feels through psychometry is stronger than mine. In the case of severe physical, emotional or sexual abuse, the personal object that Jackie holds starts to radiate heat, signaling *bad vibes*. Jackie feels strong emotions and also sees visions during these sorts of readings. Sometimes she is given messages that may sound meaningless to her but are significant to the client. Jackie's ability to wear a client's feelings can be very exhausting and terrifying. For instance, tuning into the energy of a person who has been physically or sexually violated is as intense for Jackie as it was for the client, though in Jackie's case it is brief.

As humans, we are designed to interrelate. We were not meant to exist or move through the world in a state of fear or isolation. Love and acceptance are basic emotional needs for all human beings, but people so often allow themselves to be victimized by their own fears. I have seen many clients who have come to me in the midst of an emotional crisis, unable to see any solution or way out because they have become paralyzed with fear. It is a very good sign that they have sought help because it means that it is not too late to heal this condition. When I meet a client who is aware only that they feel desperately unhappy or dissatisfied, it may be a result of a permanently retracted aura. I suggest they read the book *Feel the Fear and Do It Anyway* by Susan Jeffers. Jeffers provides effective tools and advice for escaping the trap of fear and the paralysis that may linger following severe emotional crisis.

An inverted cone-shape indicates an aura that is barely contained in the individual's body—it is already reaching for the next plane of existence. Cone-shaped auras are demonstrated by people whose spirits have evolved so far they will never have to adopt the human form again. I believe that after these individuals leave the earthly realm they will become angels. You may experience the feeling of being around these people when you meet someone you could describe as glowing with an energy that was calm, accepting and full of love. I witnessed an incredible example of this one day recently while walking through a shopping mall with Jackie. I saw a homeless, rather unkempt-looking woman with long grey hair. Because she looked poor and untidy, people looked right past her, barely noticing she was there. But I could see this woman's aura, and I was so taken aback by what I saw that

I grabbed Jackie's arm. This woman's inverted cone-shaped aura went right up through the top of the skylight of the mall. I believe she was an angel, no longer rooted in this dimension.

Whether or not you can see it or feel its effects, your aura is an integral part of you. Auras can take on layers, glow, expand, retract and vibrate; however, the base color of your aura is as constant as the color of your eyes. The color and type of aura that I most like to see is a light violet or gold one that glows from the ground to the top of the subject's head; it contains a flood of light, flowing energy and can extend several feet from the body. I find this type of aura is like the lighthouse beacon that welcomes a ship safely back to shore, guiding the weary traveler back home.

GUARDIAN ANGELS AND SPIRIT GUIDES

The best way to describe a guardian angel is that they are entities or the souls of people who once lived in the earthly sphere as human beings. After learning the lessons they needed to develop to a very high spiritual level, they crossed over to another realm. From that higher realm they can guide and protect the living. I do believe that when people die, their good work (their higher purpose) continues from the other side; they can become guardian angels to help guide the rest of us on our earthly journeys. We can call upon them in times of need, and we can also ask for their help, guidance and strength during particularly trying or distressing circumstances.

I have never met anyone who has not had at least one guardian angel. Though I don't always see them, I am able to sense their presence. I am not able to communicate with them, though sometimes they will give me their name or some detail of their lives while they were living in the earth's energy field. I cannot contact or transmit messages from people to these entities. I am not a medium. However, if they so choose, I can receive messages from them, as I did in the case of the European gentleman.

The number of guardian angels that is with you at any one time changes; when you are ill, you may have more angels watching over you. The room can get pretty crowded at times—one client came to see me accompanied by over 30 angels!

There is a discernible difference between a guardian angel and a spirit guide. When I see a separate aura next to my client's aura, I know I am witnessing the presence of a spirit guide. (This is completely different than, and not to be confused with, the negative entities I call "the greys.") A spirit guide usually turns out to be someone who was known to the client as a human being, and who has recently passed away. Spirit guides give me a different sense of presence than guardian angels. Sometimes I can clearly see their auras and even feel things about the personality they were while they were in the earthly plane. I believe this soul has not yet gone to the light and has chosen, for whatever reason, to remain on this side close to the living person for whom they act as guide. I still do not know all the reasons for this, but perhaps they will be revealed to me in time.

Because I don't usually see the guardian angels of my clients while I am doing a reading, they may make their presence known in other ways. For instance, I might feel pins and needles or something like a cold breath. Other times, it is quite the opposite; rather than a chilly pins and needles feeling, there is warmth on the back of my neck, akin to having a gentle reassuring hand placed there. Jackie reports having had similar experiences—she's even had a couple of stern taps on the back of the head from guardian angels frustrated when she has gone on a tangent during a reading!

Once I have allowed a connection through a direct line like this with spirits and guardian angels, I am often bombarded with chatter, much of which doesn't seem very significant. Even after the reading is finished, they may follow me around for a while, still chattering. Sometimes there are messages of some importance to the client, and if so, I will repeat to the client the cosmic small talk I have just heard. However, when I need to turn off the connection, the only way I can accomplish it is to surround myself with white light and ask the guide, clearly and emphatically, to please leave. I look at this minor annoyance as an occupational hazard.

I may be a psychic, but I am also only human. Even though I begin every reading with a prayer asking that the truth be allowed to come through for the client's highest purpose, there have been times when I was scared out of my wits by the newly dead! In some of my readings, I have had a spirit or guardian angel show up who was someone the client did not like when they were living in the earthly dimension. I believe that if the spirit or guardian angel was an enemy or an estranged relative, their purpose in being there may be to make amends or seek forgiveness. Forgiveness can work both ways—you can ask for it or give it in this life or in the afterlife. Life is full of lessons and sometimes we need to work extra hard to learn them.

I feel that when someone experiences a miscarriage or their child dies, the soul of the child will always be around them as a guardian angel. I have personally experienced three miscarriages and then delivered a son, Cole, who lived less than a day. I see all these little souls as gentle entities (pink or white auras) looking after my son, Carson, who was born one year after Cole's brief life.

Animals can also become guardian angels or spirit guides for people. During some readings, I have sensed their energy and even the names of pets. I believe that animal spirit guides can offer the same sort of protection and comfort as formerly-human spirit guides. During a reading for a woman, a guide who gave his name as Max made contact with me; he told me to tell the woman that he would always be with her. The woman started to cry and then told me that Max had been her dog! During its life Max had truly been her best friend. It was the first time I had ever relayed a message of love from an animal on the other side. I was a bit shocked at the time, but being an animal lover and a lifelong pet owner I am thrilled to know that there are animal spirits on the other side too.

I have briefly described auras and the nature of entities and the messages I perceive during readings. While I can't show you what I see, I have also told you how you can develop some proficiency in seeing auras. But take warning: the information and instructions provided in this book are not meant to be turned into a party game! Some readers may have already passed judgment on the beliefs I have shared. Some of you may think I am a fantasist or misguided, or worse—leading people astray. I know, however, that I share these truths with the highest regard for their power of transformation. Everyone willing to listen and apply these principles to their lives has an opportunity to change their lives for the better. The stories shared here can provide insight and clarity into your own actions and reactions, and your own qualities and faults, as well as those of others. By applying the lessons at the heart of these stories, any confusing, challenging or even joyful circumstance will offer truths and new insights that can help to bring about the best possible outcome in any situation. If you find guidance in the stories, then pass them on to others who will benefit; if you read about people who have faced trying circumstances similar to your own, then perhaps you will feel reassured that you can carry the burden through to a resolution. This is the sole purpose of introspection: to gain insight from any situation or experience so that the very highest good is achieved for all concerned.

In the following chapters I will explore many of the most common issues for which clients seek my advice. Before we begin, I will share with you the prayer I say before every reading. Though I pray to the God of my faith, please substitute whatever name or word (Universal energy, Higher Power, etc.) that feels right for you, according to your belief system. After I surround myself with white light, I say:

I thank you, God, for allowing the truth to come through me for this person's highest purpose.

Two

The Fullness Of Who You Are—Your Choices

Now faith is the assurance of things hoped for,
the conviction of things not seen
Hebrews 11:1

In today's culture, expressions like "It must be fate," or "It is destiny," are used to explain many perplexing events, circumstances or problems for which people can find no satisfactory explanation or solution. Being a psychic does not predispose me to believing that our lives on the earthly plane are pre-planned, designed and manipulated by a higher power, or even controlled by our own higher selves. Embracing a sweeping concept of fate can pave the way to fatalistic thinking or worse: passive acceptance of everything that "happens" to us with a false belief that our stories were already written before we were born. We are all born with innate gifts and abilities, but it is our free will and choices that determine how we will use those gifts to achieve a level of success in life. Smart choices, careful planning, goal-setting, perseverance and hard work are all necessary to produce positive results.

In the tarot, the Wheel of Fortune is depicted as a wheel in the sky representing destiny and inevitability. In some tarot decks, the image is of people falling from the wheel, while in others, people are riding the wheel. The interpretations of the image are vast, from surprising opportunities around the corner to reversals of fortune about to destroy the subject's life. Any one of a number of metaphors can be applied to the Wheel of Fortune: a nautical wheel by which one can navigate the storms of life; a roulette wheel that spins and stops arbitrarily, holding one's future in the balance; a vast, nameless machine in which one human life is simply a tiny cog; or the opportunity to reverse and transform anything negative that has crossed one's path into a lesson for the future.

These various metaphors boil down to one thing: the course of your life is made up of circumstances and events *plus* attitude. Though circumstances and events are often outside your control, it is your attitude that will determine the ultimate consequences of those two factors. Do you want to choose the consequences of your own life? Do you want to feel empowered? Do you believe you can take charge of your destiny, or do you feel powerless, unable to exert authority over your own life?

RECOGNIZE YOUR MOST POWERFUL TOOL

The most powerful tool that human beings possess is our freedom of choice. Our choices direct the course of our lives. Many readings show me that a client is faced with choices that will determine a chain of events reaching far into their future. It may set off a domino effect that keeps tipping over tiles for many generations. This is what I call a split path. One image that shows me the client is facing a split path is the Chariot—alternate destinies unfolding from a conscious or unconscious decision. In traditional tarot, the Chariot represents a battle that requires willpower, determination and hard work.

A client came to me recently for advice about a love triangle in which he, by design, was the pivotal point. He had fallen in love with a woman with whom he had thought he was having an unabashed fling. He had never planned to leave his wife. Now he was faced with a decision that would result, inevitably, in people, including himself, getting hurt; children on both sides of the equation would be deeply hurt. Whatever decision he made at this crossroads would reach far into his future, even into the next generation; it could even alter the fact of the existence of another generation (his new love was young enough to have more children).

His reading showed me the split path: the Chariot card of the tarot. This card, which indicates the split path or pivotal choice, is important to understand because it is universal. At some point in *everyone's* life there is a choice of which road to take. The choice that a person makes at this juncture will change their own lives and many other people's lives forever. That is why it is so important to face this split path moment with clarity and purpose. To return to this client as an example, he was suffering a tremendous burden of guilt. He had strayed from his marriage because his wife had begun having emotional problems that she didn't deal with appropriately; instead of confronting her with the fact that she was not seeking solutions but simply venting at him, he sought an escape. He still loved his wife, but he also loved the younger woman. Whom should he choose?

I examined his reading for clues that would tell me the outcome that each of his choices would bring about. I could not advise him which path to take; I could only tell him what was likely to happen in the future along each path. I told him that either choice led to significant consequences. If he chose his new love, many people whom he had loved, trusted and wanted in his life would judge him, reject him, and possibly try to punish him. However, if he stayed in his marriage, he faced the consequences of losing all the possibilities offered by a new life with someone he truly loved.

What did I advise him to do? I told him to make a decision—*any* decision. That was the critical message of his reading. Sitting on the fence, continuing his affair and fearing the consequences of choosing presented the greatest risk of all. The guilt of his lying and indecision held far more potential hazards for him than either of the other paths. Standing still at a crossroads is an impossible and dangerous position. Energy becomes blocked because it has no direction in which to flow. The result is an erosion of self-confidence and an increasingly overwhelming sense of powerlessness, which eventually can lead to physical illness. In chapter four, I will discuss the merits of choosing a spouse over a new lover and vice-versa. The important element of this example is that the individual must understand that their own actions and decisions have brought them to this crossroads. Now they must get ready to face the ultimate consequences of this choice. Failing to make a decision will lead to much greater harm than either of the paths they have before them.

ACTION PLUS ATTITUDE EQUALS OUTCOME

In a case such as the one above, making a decision leads to something greater than just the choice of power over powerlessness; it represents an opportunity to meet the problems in one's life with resilience versus resistance. The attitude you adopt when dealing with challenges, whether they are unforeseen circumstances or consequences of past decisions, will dictate the outcome. Resilience is the byproduct of a willingness to take responsibility for your actions and choices. It means that you can recover quickly from setbacks, adjusting and adapting to different environments and challenges. Everyone meets with difficult circumstances in life: resilience and willingness to work through these challenges is the path to enlightenment.

On the other hand, resistance to the lessons available through life's challenges impedes the natural flow of energy—making mental, emotional and spiritual progress slow and difficult or even impossible. Resistance is at work when there is failure to make a choice; energy stagnates until circumstances come about that will force an outcome. While we are resisting, blocked energy creates friction in other areas of our lives, or it becomes dead weight, slowing us down. Forward movement becomes strained, painful or stops altogether. When this happens, we have fallen out of step with the natural rhythm of the rest of the universe. Resilience allows us to remain in step with all of life and receptive to the solutions that can come about when energy is not blocked.

Since we are all part of the same universal energy, we

ultimately receive in accordance with what we contribute. If you constantly send negativity out into the universe, then you invite negativity into your life. Alternatively, by sending out love and positive energy, you will open your life to all the love and positive energy that will flow back to you. This is the law of attraction. It is reflected in ancient writings of many of the world's religions, including the Christian bible. In Mark 4:25, scripture tells us, "For whoever has, to him more will be given; but whoever does not have, even what he has will be taken away from him." Gratitude and generosity beget abundance, while ingratitude and greed beget scarcity.

It is easy to make this concept a natural part of your daily life. Charity encompasses so much more than gifts of money. Everyone can give the priceless gifts of time, a listening ear or a kind word. Examine any resentments and criticisms you harbor about others and ask yourself, "Is this contributing positively to the energy of the universe? Is this attitude helpful?" If the answer is no, then isn't it time to banish such negative thoughts from your way of thinking? Negative patterns—including thoughts—have an impact on the world no matter how small or seemingly insignificant. Think of an empty jug: negative thoughts are drops of water filling the jug until it overflows. Envision filling that jug with positive thoughts instead; soon the jug will be too small to hold all the positive energy available. You can be a vessel filled with positive energy and find yourself awash in a sea of positive waves that touch the lives of many others.

There is comfort in all of these things: knowing that you have the power of free will, choosing to be resilient and understanding that you are a part of the constant flow of energy in the universe.

You have the power to bring positive change and abundance into your life. In the next section of this chapter, I want to share how choices are not made only through deeds, but also in thoughts.

CHANGE YOUR PERCEPTION OF THE PAST TO CHANGE YOUR FUTURE

Many people who consult me for insight into what lies ahead are actually much less interested in their future than they are in dwelling on the past. I use the word "dwelling" because it is such an apt description of their root problem. They literally live in the past, stuck at the point in their lives where they were abandoned, shamed, betrayed, or suffered other emotional and/or physical violation. Every moment of their lives since that time has been informed by the pain of those experiences. They have arranged every thought about who they are, what they do and what they want around the nucleus of their negative experience. Their suffering has formed a wall around their point of view so that they cannot see beyond the trauma of their past. What they don't realize is that by focusing on the negative, they are drawing more negative energy into their lives. Energy attracts like energy. Negative thoughts attract negative energy. These victims of the past, though they tell themselves they want to move forward in their lives, really want a magic potion or spell that will change the past and take away the terrible injury that was done to them and all the pain associated with it.

Well, for all of you who have suffered a grievous injury in the past, here is the magic spell that will help you to change the past:

Every day just as you are waking up, *before* your mind is seized by your habitual negative thoughts, visualize your life in the present moment as a filing cabinet. Open the filing cabinet and retrieve a file containing a negative thought. For instance: "As a small child, every day I cried after my mother left me with a babysitter to go to work. If my mother had not chosen a career over staying at home to look after me as a child, I would not be suffering from the overwhelming fear that my spouse will leave me one day."

Now, replace that one negative thought with a positive one. For instance: "As a small child, every day I cried after my mother left me with a babysitter to go to work. This experience left me with a deep certainty that one day I would be left to care for myself entirely on my own. I now see this experience as a life lesson. Because I had a deep unconscious belief that I would have to look after myself, I have mastered many skills. I have developed an independent personality and confidence that comes from knowing that I am capable of taking care of myself."

This may not sound like much when you read it, but try this simple exercise and you will be amazed at the results. At first, it may help to write down all the good things in your life and keep that list of positive thoughts next to your bed; before long you won't need to read the list to recall the positive things. If you hear yourself say, "There are no good things," think again. What about all the things we so often take for granted? If you are reading this book, then you have your sense of sight. What about all your other senses, your mobility, a child (can be a nephew, niece, or friend's child), or a talent you have? One by one, replace all the files containing habitual negative thought patterns with positive ones. Before you know it, your outlook will transform from negative to positive. You will begin to notice all the good things that are part of your life, and you will welcome all experiences—even challenges—with a sense of gratitude. As a result of exuding positive energy instead of negative, you will attract even more positive energy into your life. Suddenly, you will feel lighter and more receptive; you will welcome each moment and feel grateful for *all* the lessons available in each experience.

I shared this exercise once during a reading with a client whom I will call Irene. When Irene first visited me, she was seeking help for the overwhelming feelings of anger and resentment she was experiencing against a particular individual. Though hatred is a very strong word, it was one which Irene used to describe how she felt about this man. My reading revealed that Irene had suffered a grievous wrong in her past when this man, a family friend, had molested her as a young teenager. She had never told her parents for fear it would be seen as her fault. For many years she even believed that somehow she had been to blame. Her feelings of shame grew as did the anger and hatred she felt about the man. She constantly thought about the vengeance she would like to have against him. As she got older, her view of men was that they were all capable of such terrible acts; she felt that no matter how much she loved or trusted a boyfriend or husband—eventually, she would be betrayed.

Irene's vision of that future was so strong it actually came true. She was betrayed by men over and over again. Irene's reading showed me the Devil upside down. This image represented power of the mind. I explained to Irene that her own thoughts were at the root of her negative life experiences. Only Irene had the power to change her thoughts, and by doing so, turn her life around to draw to her positive experiences. Irene left the reading angry and disappointed. She expressed her annoyance at my interpretation and what she called "blaming the victim." Once again, Irene felt as though she were being held accountable for the wrong that had been done to her; her overwhelming cloud of anger and negativity now included me.

So you will understand why I was so surprised when Irene came to see me after many years. This time it was her turn to enlighten me. She told me that she had felt blinded by anger over what she had lost. But it was not just dignity and innocence she had lost, it was peace of mind. After months of continuing to feel increasing anger over all the negative circumstances that continued to plague her, she finally decided that she had nothing to lose by trying the exercise I had described to her. One by one, she replaced her negative thoughts with positive ones. After several weeks of making this a regular practice, she felt ready to tackle the biggie, the one that started it all: "If I had not been molested, I would not be constantly choosing men who betray me." It was time to replace the file, she told herself as she read aloud the affirmation I had written down for her so many months before: "If I had not experienced the betrayal of men in the past, I would not be able to recognize the value of a good, trusting relationship." At first it did not ring true. "Where was this good trusting relationship?" she thought. But the damage her negative feelings had done was clear. And the benefits she had been experiencing with her adoption of a positive attitude were unmistakable. Irene could not give up. She was determined to replace the negative file containing her perception of the past that had infected her present and future.

Eventually it did happen. She was not only able to replace all the negative files with positive ones, but she was even able to forgive the man who had committed the original crime against her. Then she learned that the same crime had been committed against him when he was a child. Though that does not excuse his actions, it did fill her with a sense of compassion for the terrible existence he must have endured. His thoughts had been so corrupted by the trauma of his experience that he didn't recognize the monstrous wrong he was committing against another human being.

Irene was so impressed with the transformation in her life that she came back to tell me and to apologize for her reaction after the reading. I was pleased to have such firm confirmation of what I had seen in Irene's reading. Her belief that she would be betrayed by men was so intense that, without realizing it, she repeatedly created circumstances to fulfill that belief. Eventually she was able to find and maintain a healthy, loving relationship with a wonderful man. Today they continue to enjoy a happy and trusting relationship.

Some readers are undoubtedly shaking their heads and saying, "How can Kim be so smug? She has obviously never suffered the way that Irene suffered." I can tell you that I have indeed suffered grievous wrongs in my life. How do you think I was able to share that exercise with Irene and many other clients with such confidence? I could because I knew that it worked. It had worked for me.

One of the tremendous positives that came from my repeated experiences of betrayal was finally finding and appreciating Gary, the wonderful man I married seven years ago. Given my strong personality, I was always in danger of taking a good man for granted. I used to find untrustworthy men exciting. I saw their irresponsible behavior as the mark of an adventurous spirit. I can now discern between honest men who take their commitments seriously and selfish men who take what they want without considering the consequences. By replacing my own negative thought patterns with positive ones, I was able to change my perception of the past and thereby change my future.

I can tell you that this process works because I have done it for myself. Here are some affirmations to help you get started on changing your perception of the past. Write these down; read them as often as possible; even carry them with you. The constant bombardment of your psyche with negative messages of the past requires a concerted effort on your part in order to be transformed. Support your work in replacing your negative files with these positive reinforcements:

• I recognize and accept that I cannot change the past.

• I recognize and embrace the truth that only I have the power to change my perception of the past.

• I choose to change my future by changing my perception of the past.

Here is another exercise to help you to clear negative energy:

Submerge your body into a sea salt bath—use about a cup let it dissolve before you get into the bathtub. Light a white candle (making sure it is a safe distance from anything flammable). Looking into the white candle say, "I release all negative energy into the white light." As you look into a white candle, focus on surrounding yourself with white energy. If you have to do this 10 days in a row, keep doing it as often as it feels uplifting to you. You will notice that your feelings of negativity are less and less and with a little more effort to focus on the positive you can eliminate all the negative energy you are holding onto, sometimes without even knowing it.

WHAT OTHER PEOPLE THINK OF YOU IS NONE OF YOUR BUSINESS

I don't know who was first to coin this phrase, though it has been used by inspirational speakers and writers for some time. When I first heard it, I thought, "Wow. That's exactly what I've been telling my clients for years!"

We are all so worried what other people think—of us, of our spouses, of our kids, our home—of everything! Why? What has another person's private thoughts got to do with me? The existence of a thought or belief about *anything* exists only in the mind of the person having the thought—thinking something does not make it true. In fact, the thoughts that I have tell much more about me than about the subject of my thoughts. If I love or hate the color green, does it mean that green is a "good" or "bad" color? It means nothing as far as the color green is concerned; it only means that I have an opinion of the color green *based on my own history*. Maybe I had a favorite green blanket as a child; maybe I love plants; maybe I am a natural healer—any or all of these factors could contribute to a positive relationship with the color green. I am viewing green through the filter of my experiences; I relate the color green to other things that I value or use for significant purposes.

If we take the analogy one step further and replace the color green with a person—let's call her Emily—I may think to myself one day that I like Emily. In my thoughts, I comment that Emily is a good person. I may share that opinion with someone else and they may, in turn, relate it to Emily. Should Emily feel like she is a better person for the fact that *I think* she is a good person? Why would she? It doesn't *make* her a good person just because I think so. Only Emily can decide for herself whether or not she believes she is a good person. Of course, the corollary to this discussion is that only Emily can decide for herself whether or not she possesses any number of negative characteristics that may be attributed to her by other people. Only Emily can decide whether it is true that she is mean, fat, lazy, stupid ... the list might be endless. If Emily believes, in her heart, that any of this is true, then Emily needs to take the steps necessary to change these characteristics and become someone that *she* likes and enjoys living with—because she is the only one living 24–7 with Emily!

All of this might sound a little simplistic, but I cannot count the number of times I have said these words to my clients. It is not an exaggeration to say that nearly 100 percent of the people who ask my advice have fallen into the trap of accepting that what other people say about them is true—whether positive or negative—and that it matters. Only you can pass judgment on yourself. If you don't like who you are, what you are doing, how you are feeling, then you have the power to make the changes necessary. It is self-defeating to try to change what someone else thinks about you. Why? Because you cannot possibly know all the experiences, opinions, assumptions, fears and all the other filters through which their thoughts pass before they reach the conclusion that ends with an opinion about you. Even identical twins have their own private thoughts and may react differently to the same stimulus or experiences.

The important thing is to do whatever it takes to feel good about who you are. This might mean taking a hard look at your faults and admitting that you have made mistakes—every human being has! Forgive yourself, get over the embarrassment or self-deprecation, and take a step forward into the rest of your life.

You cannot change the past, but you can certainly alter your perception of the past. By changing how you view the past—your challenges, your wounds and grievances, the wrongs you have committed, any mistakes you have made—all of these are wrapped up in the personal history that has brought you to this moment. It is *this* moment that you live in, not the millions of moments (or even one) you lived before now and not the moment you will live next; this moment is the only moment you can influence. By changing your perception of the past and by living fully in this moment, you can shape your future.

I will give you an example of this as it relates to one of my clients. When Roseanne came to me for a reading, she arrived precisely on time; she was impeccably groomed, and I noticed that everything she wore was perfectly matched—shoes, purse, even nail polish. Not a hair was out of place, not an eyelash was stuck together. Roseanne was the picture of perfection. Her issue, therefore, came as a surprise even to me. Roseanne told me she desperately needed help to change her untidy appearance. I stared at her in silence, waiting for her to explain what I was clearly not seeing.

Roseanne told me briefly about her childhood spent in poverty. She had never owned a new article of clothing until she was eighteen years old and earning her own living. She had worked hard at school, put herself through college and was now a legal assistant for a large downtown firm. No matter how hard she tried, she could not shake the sense that people constantly scrutinized her for the cleanliness and neatness of her appearance. Because of this, no matter what she did, she felt untidy. Even a hair out of place set off a storm of self-doubt and the feeling that "everyone is looking at me."

The appearance of The Moon in Roseanne's reading showed the illusion she had constructed from which she looked out at the world. The most crippling weight on Roseanne's shoulders was her own mistaken belief that others judged her and found her wanting. Instead of seeing her reflection in a mirror as others truly saw her, Rosanne's overwhelming sense of shame regarding her poor beginnings eclipsed any positive self-image she might have developed. Even her obsessive attention to her appearance did not satisfy her internalized critical voice. My advice to Roseanne was to take immediate steps toward releasing her self-image from the prison of her past. Though it would be a long journey to replace all the negative self-talk that had lodged itself in her mind, Roseanne could never hope to build a happy life until she raised her self-esteem.

The day you stop thinking about what anyone thinks of you is the day your own mind will be free. Your anxieties concerning what everyone else thinks about you will no longer consume and control your own thoughts. Can you imagine for just a moment the freedom you will feel? Think of how much more you will smile and laugh, how much easier it will be to meet new people, how much harder it will be to stay angry at anyone and how seldom you will ever stand in judgment of anyone else or their actions.

Don't you want to be that free, enlivened, self-assured person right now? Make the choice to free yourself from the burden of carrying around anybody else's opinion of you—good or bad.

I have been sharing some of the side benefits that come with changing old ways of thinking and adopting new behaviors; this one is no exception. There are too many side benefits to list; however, one of the most crucial is that the moment you shift your focus from what other people think of you is the moment that everyone else stops making snap judgments. Once you become a person who clearly approves of himself/herself, guess what? The rest of the world jumps on board! When you feel that much certainty about the person you are, when you stop trying to win the approval of others, your aura opens up. The energy you project becomes inviting; people feel good just being around you; you are sought out for your good company and happy disposition. And though you are no longer concentrating—or caring—about what other people think, their thoughts about you are positive; with that much good energy surrounding you, even your faults (we all have them) are overlooked. But don't get complacent. Remember to *be* as caring, thoughtful and kind as you appear to be.

Three

Career Choices

A joyful heart is good medicine, but a
broken spirit dries up the bones.
Proverbs 17:22

The focus of this chapter is to explore the vocational predispositions that I see in auras and what the tarot shows me. By sharing some of the real stories of clients who have consulted me on career choices, it is my hope that readers who seek guidance regarding their profession or choice of jobs, or those who want to understand a persistent restlessness that seems to pervade every job they've ever had, might get a glimpse of a possible future that includes more rewarding career or education choices. Case studies will hopefully inspire you to look at work and education in a whole new way.

To find and follow your calling is a lifelong journey that requires courage, self-confidence and conscious design. As with any journey, it begins with the first step. Your first step will be to define—or re-define your talents, strengths, abilities and interests.

Without identifying what these are for you *today*, which may result in some surprise changes over your past conclusions, how can you possibly expect to prepare yourself for what lies ahead?

AURAS, ABILITIES AND PERSONALITY TRAITS

In order for happiness and energy to flow effortlessly, we need to live in alignment with our own natural traits, abilities and talents. We are all born with certain character traits and predispositions, some of which may be apparent at an early age. Studies have indicated that the areas of natural interest for children between the ages of four and six were most often the areas where they demonstrated their keenest abilities in adulthood. By recognizing and nurturing these early inclinations, we may be able to realize a more fulfilling career path.

Observing auras has often helped me to provide guidance regarding my clients' career choices and decisions. Certain colors indicate natural abilities and characteristics that fit particular careers. Factors indicated by aura colors are often echoed by the tarot images that appear in a client's reading. I must stress, however, that there is no precise formula that can be applied to the tarot images that I interpret. The advice or, more accurately, the language of auras and the tarot that I translate for clients is based as much on the meaning behind the images and aura colors as the feelings I perceive around the client, the cards, and the circumstances reflected in the tarot layout. Though I refer here to a layout, as mentioned earlier, my readings are done by a method I developed using blocks instead of traditional tarot cards. The Di-Cerot Tarot Blocks provide me with an almost three-dimensional viewpoint of the client's past, present and future choices.

As previously noted, blue auras are generally associated with grounded and stable people who are most happy in the planning and construction industries; they need to see tangible results of their actions and hard work.

Gold and white auras are indicative of helpers or teachers. Readings for these clients often show the Empress image in the place of career, which is a card I often associate with social work, a career suited to personality types who derive satisfaction from helping others. However, I see many of these caring, industrious people struggle with the challenge of separating their work from their personal lives. This might be indicated in a reading that shows the Empress surrounded by clubs or the Devil reversed, which indicates the inability to separate one's personal life from one's work life.

Succeeding in a career where you are constantly faced with the problems of other people requires the strength to listen to those problems, provide guidance and leadership in resolving or accepting issues, and then leaving those problems and clients behind at the end of the work day. Unfortunately, for many who choose this line of work the boundaries between their personal and business lives becomes blurred. They are unable to view the burdens of others objectively and end up shouldering those burdens themselves. This can create many problems in their own lives, including burnout, fatigue and feelings of failure or being overwhelmed by life. This may show up as the Five of Clubs, a card that indicates weariness from taking on too much or carrying the burdens of others.

Whether you are pursuing a paid career in a helping profession or serving as a volunteer in a helping capacity, it is crucial to maintain an objective viewpoint. Taking on the problems of others as if they are your own will only serve to defeat you and will throw your energy into imbalance. In order to perform in a healthy way in this type of work, you must develop the ability to listen and to empathize, but not internalize, other people's issues and challenges. If you are not able to separate your job from the rest of your life, then you will absorb the pain and grief of others and, ultimately, make it your own. This can, in turn, become physical illness: pain in the neck, back, or shoulders can be the manifested troubles of others that you carry around with you. More importantly, you are leaving your own path to wander down a path that isn't even yours!

If this describes your career situation, then you will benefit from taking time to simply stop what you are doing and examine all your motivations. Are you becoming absorbed in the lives of others because you have failed to develop your own personal interests? Have you sacrificed opportunities for recreation, artistic pursuits or personal development because you are too busy fixing the lives of others? Do your tireless efforts on behalf of other people mask a reluctance to deal with your own shortcomings in the area of relationships, creating a home or achieving satisfaction through work, whether paid or unpaid? Though your efforts and dedication to your career may be applauded by some, sacrificing your own path can never be seen as the best application of your time, skills or talents. By taking the time to stop and ask yourself hard questions about why you may be using your work to avoid creating a satisfying life of your own, you can change this behavior before it manifests as physical illness.

Other images in the tarot indicate particular careers or

vocations: the Justice card shows me a client is involved in or drawn to the legal field, while The Hierophant represents someone working in an institution such as a hospital or university. Workers in government are often indicated by Pages of any suit, but particularly the Page of Pentacles. These personality types enjoy following instructions and thrive in jobs where their duties adhere to formal or even rigid guidelines. Their auras usually show shades of blue and white.

When I see an orange aura around someone, it tells me loud and clear that this person needs to do something creative to keep their energy flowing. Writing, art, acting, architecture, interior decorating, even doing hair, make-up and nails, fall under the creativity umbrella. When I do readings for an individual with an orange aura who is not working at a job with a creative mandate, I may see them as depressed, empty and feeling hopeless; for a creative person, being trapped in a non-creative job can mean death to the soul. Interestingly, the client may appear to all observers as though they are cheerful, enthusiastic and content with their lives. The client, however, experiences nagging doubts, frequent bouts of listlessness or a general sense that their lives are somehow not right. They have come to me to help them identify this undefined sense of dissatisfaction.

It does not always require leaving a well-paid job in order to create a greater sense of satisfaction or fulfillment in your life. Often, a client only needs to balance an otherwise healthy career life by serving an unmet creative urge. A persistent sense that they are missing out on something can be transformed into a satisfying creative outlet, regardless of whether or not it generates an income. If an individual with an orange aura has a well-paid job that is in a non-creative field, I may advise them to take creative courses at night or on the weekends so that they will have an outlet for their blocked creative energy.

I am reminded of a reading that I did for Bill, whose aura was predominantly orange. Bill was in the finance business (which some people say can be creative!) and making loads of money, but he felt unfulfilled. He was honest and hardworking, but no matter how much success he achieved, he was not happy; he felt depressed and drained of his zest for life. Bill also happened to be a fabulous dancer. After a reading where I learned about his passion for dancing, I encouraged Bill to satisfy his natural inclinations without leaving his successful career. After talking about it, Bill had a better understanding of the source of his unhappiness. He no longer felt foolish about pursuing his love of dance. Bill took lessons at night and on weekends, and whenever he could find the time he would dance. By releasing his passion for dance, Bill was able to break through the blockage that had dammed his energy. He kept his job in the financial field, but his love and expression of creativity through dance helped to keep his energy flowing, which resulted in even greater success in his career.

Sacrificing a secure job and a regular paycheck to dive headfirst into a new, unknown career is not the typical advice I give to clients. However, in Richard's case it was the correct move to make. At the time that Richard came to me, he was employed in a job that paid reasonably well, but offered little stimulation. Richard could see ahead to a lifetime of boredom with little to look forward to beyond a secure pension. His reading showed me the Hanged Man: someone who is suspended upside down by one foot. This is an individual who is stuck, literally hanging on for dear life. His energy is not flowing, but he is afraid to take the risk required to claim his true vocation.

Richard's reading also showed that he possessed exceptional talent. When I asked him if he was aware of any innate talents he had, he told me that he had been told many times that he had a gift for comedy, music and acting. He had always wanted to pursue a career in the entertainment field, but like many who find themselves in a similar position, he was afraid to take the risk. For Richard, however, the risk was not so much in giving up his security; what he felt was at risk was the loss of his dream. "What if he failed?" he asked me; what would his family and friends think of him? Would they lose faith in his talent? How would he carry on knowing that he had failed and worse, that his beloved dream was lost forever? As long as it was unattainable, Richard reasoned, the dream stayed alive in his own mind.

There are three important factors to take into account when looking at pursuing creativity. The first is that creative success does not always equal fame and fortune. Millions of talented writers, actors and musicians have long, productive and rewarding careers in relative obscurity. They are, however, doing what they really want to do. The second factor is that following your dream takes persistence that may not pay off for a while, but even famous people had to start somewhere. For instance, superstar Brad Pitt started out dressed as a chicken, promoting the Pollo Loco restaurant chain. There are multitudes of similar examples.

The third and most important factor is recognizing that failure is not the end of the world. On the other hand, looking back on a lifetime of missed opportunity can be truly tragic. If sacrificing the security of a job is too great a risk, consider asking for a leave of absence or find a way to pursue your dream career in stages. In other words, commit yourself to the dream, researching and planning a strategy for achieving milestones of success. However, diminish the risk to your livelihood by putting a back-up plan in place. Later in this chapter, I offer additional suggestions for making a gradual transition toward a more satisfying career.

Recognize that no matter how cherished your dream may be, if you don't pursue it, the regrets you may experience later on may feel like a more profound loss than if you had tried and failed. Accept that the dream might not become reality but developing courage, determination and faith in yourself will be hidden benefits of your genuine efforts.

Predisposition is not the only critical element in determining the path of greatest work-related satisfaction. In Richard's reading, his talent in the entertainment field was accompanied by a combination of the Wheel of Fortune and the Ten of Cups (or Ten of Coins), coupled with strong cards—Kings (or Queens). This was an indication that Richard had the potential to attract a large audience. In this type of reading, the audience may not be in the field of entertainment; it can also be in sports, journalism, public speaking, politics—anything that puts the individual in the public eye. I will encourage the subject to take the necessary risks to get out into the limelight when a combination shows tremendous potential for success.

I recall a reading I did for Rebecca, whose son, Guy, a medical student, appeared in her reading represented by a Page of Pentacles. The surrounding cards showed that though he was studying hard and succeeding, he was not in the line of study where he would find his greatest potential for success. Rebecca's cards showed that instead of becoming a physician, Guy's true destiny lay in research. An opportunity was about to arise for Guy that would lead to the development of a cure for a widespread disease. Shortly after Rebecca's reading, the students in one of Guy's classes at medical school were asked to volunteer for a new research project. Rebecca had told her son about her reading and whether or not Guy trusted the accuracy of the reading, he certainly trusted the potential for his mother's disapproval if he passed up this opportunity. Some time later, Rebecca contacted me to tell me that through the research project Guy had participated in, he had inadvertently happened upon a potential cure for a common, debilitating disease.

If the Four of Coins appears in a reading, the message is that I am reading an individual who is content with their life and work. This satisfaction can also be shown by the appearance of the Ace of Cups, indicating inspired creativity and a passion for life. Unfortunately, only about 10 percent of the clients I read have these cards. Many more people that I do readings for dislike what they do. This doesn't necessarily mean that they don't enjoy their work; it can mean that the environment they work in is not healthy or inspiring. Many of these people feel they are victims of temporary circumstances, resigned to putting in time until something better comes along. Hopefully, their assessment of the brevity of their situation is correct.

Other people who seek my advice regarding their employment situation are fully aware of how unhappy they are with their jobs. In some cases, "unhappy" is an enormous understatement.

These individuals resent every day and hour they spend at their jobs. This constant loathing manifests in their auras as blockages around either the third (stomach) or fifth (throat) chakras often accompanied by dark red retracted auras. Constant bombardment of the mind, body and soul with negative thoughts and resentment often manifests into disease. This means that not only will these individuals feel trapped in jobs they resent; in this state, they offer an open invitation to illness as well.

What is the solution to such a dilemma? The road back to emotional and physical health is a challenging one, but take heart, because there is a way out. With perseverance, this journey can be the most satisfying undertaking that you will ever embrace. Altering our chosen path is extremely hard work, often fraught with obstacles that loom so large we want to run for cover. We may question why we headed down this path of redemption in the first place. But finding our way back from an unfulfilling career choice can lead to greater happiness than we ever thought possible.

Dean was a divorced man with two children at home when he came to see me. He worked hard at his job as produce manager at a local grocery store, but Dean had a dream of being a paramedic. At 42 years old he had a family to raise and other commitments; taking a new road was not going to be easy. Dean applied himself—doing everything he could to attain his dream. He still worked during the day and provided for his children, but he took night courses and even used the equity in his home to cover his costs during his final year of full-time studies. After years of believing it was possible, Dean finished the program, achieving excellent final marks. His commitment to hard work and to his dream paid off. With his good record behind him, Dean was offered an exciting job as a paramedic for an airline, escorting travelers who were too ill or injured to travel alone. Today Dean travels the world helping people, and more importantly, he loves his work.

I found Dean's drive and ambition an absolute inspiration and recount his story often to those wondering if they can find more meaning in their lives by making different choices. I say, "Yes, you can." You need to maintain a long-term goal that you keep constantly in sight along the way. During the difficult times, you will need reminders for why you began this adventure of change and growth. You also need to create attainable short-term goals. As you achieve each of these short-term goals you will feel your motivation renewed and your confidence boosted.

I am reminded of a reading I did for Angela, a successful financial planner. She seemed to have it all: the beautiful home, a loving and successful husband, and two beautiful children enrolled in private school. I was envious of the woman who sat in front of me, until I saw what the tarot showed me. The reading was full of negative images: the Devil, and the Chariot and clubs together, signifying leaving home angry, and the Hanged Man in the centre of her career layout. In short, the tarot showed that though she was successful at her job, she felt miserable and trapped by her work. Every morning when the alarm clock went off, she was gripped with tension and anxiety, feelings that persisted throughout every work day.

As with most people, Angela's reading was not all negative. It also showed that she possessed tremendous creative ability. This was confirmed by the orange I could see in her aura. I asked her about her interests as a child and she told me how she used to spend many happy hours in her grandmother's huge garden. When I suggested that she take courses in floral design, she almost fell off her chair; she knew that she had a talent for floral design, and it had always been her secret dream to work with flowers. She had never shared this dream with anyone, not even her husband; it had seemed so foolish compared with the high-powered executive status she had become accustomed to as a senior financial planner.

Angela had felt embarrassed, even afraid to tell her husband that she wanted to leave her excellent job to open a florist business. She felt that exposing her secret dream in that way left her open to ridicule. In the same way that Richard had done, Angela rationalized that as long as it remained a secret, it was still possible. I pointed out the obvious flaw in Angela's reasoning: as long as it remained a secret, it remained an unlived dream!

After the reading, Angela felt encouraged. I had not ridiculed or minimized her longing for a creative outlet, even though it would mean stepping down from the corporate world into a career requiring long hours, hard work and careful planning to succeed. Rather than having her dream crushed by exposure, it was if she had received a nod from a higher source—her own soul—telling her that it was not only acceptable to go for her dream, it was necessary in order to feel fulfilled. Angela made significant adjustments to her lifestyle and personal finances, including sacrifices she had not anticipated. But the trade-off was worth it. In exchange for the material goods she gave up, she gave herself the best gift of all: a healthier outlook, career satisfaction and the gratification of not having missed out on her dream. The unanticipated side benefit was a renewed vitality in her marriage: Angela glowed with life in her new career and that enthusiasm spread to all areas of her family and home life.

Do you share some of Angela's and Dean's feelings of disappointment in your career? Do you start the work day wishing you could be somewhere else, doing other work that would give you greater satisfaction? Everyone has bad days at their job, but if you persistently experience these feelings of dissatisfaction, there is an exercise in the Appendix at the end of this book that will help you to get clear about your career choices.

The gifts of self-love and self-awareness are available to everyone. You can give these gifts to yourself; you have permission to make quality of life a priority. You do have the power to choose to *not* spend your life chasing the almighty dollar and acquiring "stuff" with the flawed thinking that money and things will fulfill you. If you feel that somewhere along the way you made a choice that was not in harmony with your deepest dreams, desires and talents, take an honest look at your life to see where you can make healthy changes. If a drastic career change like Angela's and Dean's is what you genuinely believe is necessary, consider the short-term goals you need to realize in order to make it happen. Are there things or places that you can trim back in order to make room for your dream? Once you begin to focus on your true desires, you will find that there are many options out there to help you make the dream a reality. You may be able to arrange a four-day work week or a shared job; part-time and flex-time are becoming increasingly acceptable choices for employers who recognized that a happier employee is a higher-functioning employee. If you need time to re-think your choices in an even larger way, consider a sabbatical. Don't let habit or convention limit your possibilities. Simply living within your means will help to get you out of the money rat race. As comedian Lily Tomlin commented about the rat race, "Even if you win, you're still a rat."

If you need support in making these changes in your life, seek out others who share your views. There are many resources available on the internet that will help you to focus on what is really important in your life.

If you realize you have made a mistake in choosing your career, don't be afraid to turn around and explore alternate routes. Our lives today are very different from our grandparents' era, when 40 years of loyalty to one company was expected and the reward of a handshake and a watch was enough. We recognize that advances in science, technology and, perhaps most importantly, self-fulfillment have made career satisfaction a significant component of a well-lived life.

There are many things that you can do to move in a different direction while still maintaining your current employment. You can go to night school or take courses online or on weekends. It will demand sacrifices and some risk, but with perseverance, you will achieve the happiness that you know is possible. There will also be many rewards along the way. Each step toward your revised career goal will feel like a tremendous achievement. Every positive accomplishment toward that goal will reinforce your decision and add fuel to your determination. Keep your eyes on the goal. Envision how you will feel once you have achieved it. At every opportunity, think of how your life will be once you have adopted the career that is better suited to your talents and interests. Constantly holding that vision before you is the key to maintaining momentum. Your vision of the future will also help to diminish any nagging doubts or anxiety that will inevitably creep in to threaten your plan of the new and improved future.

Fear of change affects everyone. I talk to single moms who are working to support their families and stuck in low-paying jobs with no future. They long for change; they recognize that the path they are following can only lead to growing dissatisfaction or even despair, but they are too afraid of the risks involved in pursuing alternate career paths. With a family depending on them, they are understandably afraid that venturing outside their passionless but reliable employment could mean the loss of that small but steady paycheck. This is a situation where tremendous courage and support from family and friends can make all the difference. With support, these individuals can find the courage to invest in themselves; by achieving success, they demonstrate to their children the power of believing in goals and in their own abilities. There is no better example for a child than to watch his/her parent reach for and accomplish a lofty goal. The sacrifices along the way are insignificant in comparison with the feelings of satisfaction that are experienced day after day in a job that utilizes one's talents and abilities.

Often, the circumstances we find ourselves in are not the real challenge: it is our response to the challenges we face that determines our capacity for personal growth. One excellent example of overcoming challenges and reaping unforeseen benefits was Carolyn, a single mother living on government benefits. With few marketable skills, Carolyn felt intimidated at the prospect of entering the job market. Convinced that her children needed her to set an example, she sought my help in escaping the feelings of dependency, hopelessness and inadequacy that overwhelmed her at the thought of finding employment. Carolyn told me she had always been interested in aesthetics. Her reading showed me a Page of Pentacles, revealing a shy but determined character, accompanied by the Queen of Pentacles, indicating the ability to work hard to accomplish goals. I told Carolyn that it was certainly possible for her to escape the cycle of financial dependency, which she resented, but it would require careful planning and commitment on her part. At that moment, with confirmation that an alternative was possible, a plan began to emerge for Carolyn.

Carolyn began by setting short-term goals, beginning with earning extra money from babysitting, which she saved in a separate account designated for her long-term dream of attending cosmetology school. Other opportunities arose, such as occasional housecleaning or pet-sitting jobs. Carolyn worked hard, saving every penny that was not needed for basic living expenses, and giving up any small personal treats she might previously have allowed herself. Her diligence and determination eventually paid off. After some years, Carolyn had saved enough money to take the courses she needed to land a part-time job while she completed the program and earned her diploma. She freed herself from the long-time burden of government assistance.

Eventually, Carolyn was hired by a busy salon, and with her positive outlook and self-appreciation, she easily developed a loyal clientele. Her long-term goal of employment grew to owning and operating her own salon and not surprisingly, she accomplished her goal. In fact, she not only opened her own salon, she bought and furnished a comfortable, beautiful home. Carolyn is a real example of someone who broke through fear and entrenched attitudes to achieve her career goal and her dreams. By setting short-term and long-term goals and taking steps toward attaining them, Carolyn redefined her future. In doing so, she set an example for her children to follow. But the first step for Carolyn was the biggest—by putting a humble plan in place, she was able to overcome her fear and conquer her feelings of inadequacy. Achieving each step of the plan helped to reinforce her goals with the ultimate result that she was eventually able to accomplish enormous life changes. The entire outcome, however, would not have been possible without those first tentative steps.

Carolyn's story shows that hard work and determination is needed to reach goals. This may be a practical fact, however, it is important to recognize the side benefits that Carolyn experienced. So many people want everything to be easy. Hard work, perseverance and long-term goals simply do not fit with our modern expectations of immediate gratification. But the character-building that Carolyn experienced was as great a benefit as the achievement of her employment and financial goals. By committing herself to a long-term goal and accomplishing it, Carolyn developed a lasting belief in her own abilities. She proved herself to her toughest critic—Carolyn. In doing so, she gained self-confidence and feelings of self-worth that would not have surfaced from a quick-fix scheme. Even winning a lottery would not have provided Carolyn with the character-building experiences that served as a foundation for Carolyn's improved opinion of herself. Though Carolyn identified her goal as financial independence, the achievement of self-love was the real prize. It is important to realize that while many life circumstances seem wholly unfair, there are times when meeting the challenges life throws at us *are* the lesson. Carolyn is a prime example of meeting both inner and outward goals.

In another example, that of Patty, we can see a complete turnaround brought about by this individual's commitment to better herself. Patty was a single mother of two who worked in a series of low-paid jobs, subsisting just above the poverty line. With no assistance from the children's father, she often had to rely on food banks and public assistance for the basic necessities of life. Patty felt she was stuck on a hamster wheel going round and round, relying on government handouts when her hard work was not enough to make ends meet. Patty was determined to better herself and to create a more hopeful environment for her children. After hearing about an online program in Sociology, Patty seized the opportunity to complete her studies through a government-sponsored program offering free internet time. Patty now works for a government health and welfare department—the same people who had helped her out when she needed it most. Patty was uniquely equipped to apply her acquired knowledge and skills with real life experiences, providing her with invaluable insight into the needs of men and women in similar situations. Her empathy and first-hand knowledge provided an understanding of poverty that could not be taught. Once again, the difficulties Patty experienced as a struggling single mother were not experiences she would have sought out; however, by committing to making a change in her situation,

Patty was able to transform those challenges into valuable life lessons that benefitted herself and others.

FEAR OF CHANGE

There is an old saying: "Better the devil you know than the devil you don't know." Fear of not knowing the devils out in the world can keep us stranded in an oppressive, unhappy situation. You may not know them, but those devils have names: fear of not finding another job, fear of financial loss or ruin or of ending up in even worse circumstances. Fear of change is normal and universal, but it should not become the reason that you turn your back on opportunity. Change is a necessary and inevitable part of life, so the best way to handle it is to face it, understand it and accept it. In today's world of constant innovation, based on averages, we can expect to change careers at least four times. This means that while you are grappling with upheaval, you can take comfort in knowing that a few million other people around the world are doing the same thing: managing change.

Sometimes when I do readings for people they have the attitude that it is just too late to make a change in their career or to go back to school. I remember one man in particular who really wanted to return to school to finish his bachelor's degree. When I offered encouragement for his dream, he said, "I can't go back to school now. I will be 50 by the time I finish the program!" I reminded him that he would be 50 with or without the time put into obtaining his degree. Time marches on, with or without you.

The fear of launching a late start is shared by many people. In fact, the thought of making major mid-life changes can paralyze people with fear. I met Karen, a widow in her early 60s, who came to me feeling lost and abandoned after her husband's sudden passing. Karen had been totally dependent on her husband since they were married over 30 years earlier. "He was my world," she told me. She asked me how she could pick up the pieces of herself that she had allowed to drop when she became a young wife.

Even though Karen's husband had left her financially secure, she felt that she had no purpose in life. Karen and I discussed the grieving process and she told me that she had already been through grief counseling and she did not feel that grieving the loss of her husband was the root of her problem. She told me that with no sense of purpose in her life, she felt no compelling reason to get up in the morning. She had become so depressed that she went for days without ever leaving her house. She had stopped answering phone calls from friends, knowing that their concern for her emotional health would challenge her behavior and force her to confront her feelings of despair and hopelessness. She recognized that she was on a downward spiral, but felt powerless against her overwhelming sense that she had waited too long to reclaim her life.

After a few moments with the tarot blocks where I showed Karen images of The World, representing all that the material world has to offer and the Four of Pentacles, showing balance in her choices of career, Karen argued out loud with herself, not me, saying, "It's too late for me." When I showed her the inevitable outcome—the card of Strength, self-explanatory in this case, The Hermit, which indicated walking the right path, The Wheel of Fortune indicating events and circumstances going her way, and the Queen of Cups, representing self-discovery, Karen realized that it was only her attitude that kept her confined. She decided that it was not too late; she still had much to offer to herself, her friends and the world. She enrolled in a creative writing class offered at her local community college, and she loved it! She discovered a talent she had never known she had. She submitted some of her stories to local papers and magazines and was thrilled to see them in print. From there, she went on to write and publish stories for children. Life is no longer passing Karen by; she has reclaimed her life and though it is very different from the life she had enjoyed with her husband, Karen feels she is living to the fullest. She continues to explore new creative directions, even moving into songwriting and musical productions for theatre. I share Karen's story as proof that it is never too late to pursue self-fulfillment.

FINDING WORK OF VALUE IS YOUR JOB

While I have auras and the tarot to help me to reveal a client's abilities, you need to find other ways to define your ideal job. If your talents or gifts are obvious—if you have musical talent or a natural ability for languages, then it is easier to discover the sort of work that would best suit you. For others, honing in on areas of interest can generate feelings of frustration, confusion and doubt. Not knowing what they want is precisely what lands so many people in jobs that don't satisfy them. How can you possibly take steps to get what you want when you don't even know *what* you want?

The simplest way to begin to tune in on your abilities and interests is to think back to childhood. What was the question most frequently asked by adults when they first met you? "What do you want to be when you grow up?" Do you recall any of your answers? Did the answer evolve over the years, or change weekly, or was there a single-mindedness to your aspirations?

 Write this down: What were your favorite toys, hobbies and school subjects? Think back to collections you may have spent years in accumulating and poring over. Did you collect stamps, bits of nature, beach glass; or perhaps you collected friends the way that other people collect things—if so, write down any names you can recall.

 You can also use the process of elimination to help you in your journey to find your future life. Think about all the different occupations available today. Are there aspects of some of these jobs that you would strongly dislike? Why? Is it because the job is done indoors, outdoors, is repetitious, or requires long hours working alone? Or does it require dealing with too many people, something which pushes you out of your comfort zone? All of these factors on their own may seem insignificant, but each can play an important role in your choice of occupation. You can also consider which world events are particularly significant for you; perhaps there is a product you have used that you find frustrating enough that you would consider devoting time and energy to improve it.

 Sometimes our most obvious strengths or talents can be the very things we miss. Enlist the help of friends and family to help you uncover some of your hidden potential. My sister Nicole loves to play a game called, "If I was in charge of your life ..." Nicole is a very observant and objective person; she can zero in on an obvious match of talent and career. For example, she might say, "If I ran your life you would go into politics because you are a natural speaker, you can relate to people from every walk of life and you have natural charisma." Ask a friend or family member what job they think would suit you best; they may see a talent or trait that is well-suited to a career you never considered. There is a big red flag here—don't play this game when it comes to advising people about their relationships!

If you would rather have a completely unbiased opinion of your potential, you may learn something by taking a personality or strengths test. These are available online or you may find one offered at a local college or by a career counselor. These tests are informative and can offer good insight because the outcome cannot be manipulated by false answers. Each question will offer you several choices, such as: I work best in a realistic and investigative environment; or, I work best under pressure; and so on. Your answers will open the door to potential career paths that you can investigate further. There are literally thousands of career choices out there, many of which you might not have known existed. Often the results of strengths tests are surprising, offering options that you may not have considered. The bottom line is, when it comes to choosing a career path, you need to thoroughly explore every side street and alleyway—leave no gate or door unopened.

Perhaps you are a recent high school graduate seeking to continue your education. The number of choices available can be overwhelming. Again, leave no stone unturned; you are planning your future, so investigate all the opportunities available. Which institutions offer courses at a level that is suited to your needs? You are about to make one of the biggest purchases of your life, so be a smart consumer and research everything. This means visiting the schools wherever possible, talking to professors, former and current students, and the admissions counselor. Ask lots of questions. You can only make an informed decision when you have all the information.

If you are moving from high school into higher education, it is crucial that you choose your education and career path based on your own interests. I have seen many young people make decisions about which school to attend based on proximity to a boyfriend or girlfriend, or which school has a reputation for the best parties. The European concept of a gap year spent traveling following high school is an idea that North Americans might do well to embrace. Exploring the world is an excellent way for young people to begin the voyage of self-discovery while also learning self-reliance.

Bear in mind the big difference that exists between working at an unskilled job and taking a year out to see the world. When a young person takes a year off from school to earn money as an unskilled laborer—just to spend their money recklessly—they are apt to find themselves stuck in a rut of working to pay off their party bills. They may leave home right after high school to get a taste of freedom, only to find they have to keep working at the local food market to pay rent and buy food. This is not to minimize the value of earning a living and paying one's own way. But you must give careful thought to your choices before you make them.

Family pressures can also come into play when it is time to make decisions about formal education and career paths. Young people may be burdened by the expectations placed on them to uphold a traditional family profession or to take over a family business, whether or not they enjoy it. I have counseled many people who have regrets over years spent in the wrong line of work. I strongly advise people to be brutally honest with themselves, their family members and significant others about whether or not the family business, trade or profession is a right fit for them. Remember, if you are an individual with a powerful orange aura, there is no way that you will be happy in the family dry cleaning business.

Formal education is not the only path to success; I have given many readings where my client has achieved their financial and career goals without the benefit of a formal education. Successful entrepreneurs and sales people do not necessarily have university degrees. Many trade workers, whether or not they have pursued higher education, find their work both satisfying and financially rewarding; hard work and a willing attitude will help you accomplish more in life than a wall covered by diplomas.

As mentioned earlier, the days of a single lifetime career are largely over. Job titles and descriptions have also changed: one-word career titles such as doctor, lawyer or teacher are inadequate to describe the vast set of skills needed to perform in some jobs. A newspaper I read recently identified one spokesperson as a Managing Director of Litigations and Investigations Specializing in Quantification of Economic Damages. Phew, say that fast three times!

If you are seriously considering a change of career direction you must think about all the aspects of work that you have already done. What tasks about each of your jobs did you most enjoy? What personal strengths did you identify; what jobs best met your short and long-term personal goals? Be flexible, plan, re-plan and assess; these are all key elements on the path to finding career fulfillment. By marketing your previous experience and education in a way that garners the attention of potential employers you can land that dream job.

Keep in mind that career decisions are often heavily laden with the modern world's obsession with money and material possessions. If you want to do the work you love and feel happy and fulfilled, then you must examine your priorities. Are you the type of person who needs to own every new gadget or technological wonder? Do you crave the latest of everything from home fashions to hairstyles? Do you feel compelled keep up with the Jones's? Are there material goods beyond basic necessities that you would be willing to sacrifice in order to free up your ability to make choices about the kind of work you want to do? By refusing to respond automatically to the impulse to consume, you might widen your sphere of choices for types of work and when and where you will work.

Stop and think about this: if you were to re-evaluate your lifestyle at this moment, what elements of your life could really live without? You would be surprised by doing this exercise regularly, how much wider your net of potential opportunities would grow. Think of all the stress that would be lifted from your life if your choices were made consciously, rather than out of habitual adherence to a lifestyle you are working to uphold.

LIVING IN SYNC

We have all experienced a sense that something isn't right. I have been in business partnerships that were fraught with resistance and suspicion. When you feel that the energy in a venture is off, or that the project is not working out for you, chances are that you are right. Perhaps it is simply the wrong timing, but possibly the whole project is a wrong fit for you. If this turns out to be true, it is a lesson, though not always a lesson we want to learn. The best thing to do in this case is to acknowledge the disappointment and move on. In other words—get over it. Failing once or twice or even three times doesn't mean you must never try again.

We have all suffered disappointments. I am not exempt from these experiences. In 1999, my sister Jackie and I started a small software design company to develop a program that taught people all about football. After we obtained major sponsorship of our program from national brands, the project started to gain momentum; big dreams were born. Branching out into other sports, we received sponsorship approval from the NFL (it became the official learning CD ROM of the NFL), the NHL, the FIFA Woman's World Cup and NASCAR. Full of excitement and enthusiasm, Jackie and I traveled to a trade show in California to promote our wonderful new product.

We were little fish in a great sea of very big fish, and it showed. Our lack of experience led to trusting the wrong people, which ultimately destroyed our business. When you are watching your dream crumble to bits around you, it is hard to see the lesson right in front of you. Years later, I can see that experience as a tremendous learning opportunity, rather than a failure. It taught me more than years of formal education would have done. I learned how the market works and the importance of thinking one step ahead of everyone else in the business; how important trust and communication are in a business; and the fact that positive thinking and persistence is not enough—you also need smart planning. If you reflect on and learn from difficult situations, you can use even bad experiences to improve your life.

Another example of this can be seen in the experience of a client I will call Jean. Widowed suddenly at the age of 35, Jean was left with three children to raise on her own. Jean had never worked outside the home and though she found a reasonably well-paying job, the salary she needed to support herself and her children adequately was not easily achieved. In order to earn extra money, Jean worked nights selling clothes at home-parties. Eventually, Jean set up her own clothing manufacturing business with a partner she knew and trusted. But there was an unexpected twist: after two years in business, her partner got greedy. Unbeknownst to Jean, funds from the company were being siphoned off into a private bank account. It didn't take long for Jean's business to fail.

In spite of learning the truth about her partner's betrayal, Jean did not take legal action. Instead, she plunged her energies once again into building a company from the ground up. This time, Jean relied on her innate business sense and hired a competent chartered accountant to maintain the financial end. Jean could have focused a great deal of energy pursuing the stolen funds, but in the process, she may have sacrificed the opportunity to start again. Her decision to take the lesson and move on turned out to be a better use of her valuable time and effort.

If you have experienced disappointments similar to these examples, you must honestly examine your business idea and acumen to decide whether the venture is a good fit with your ambitions and abilities. If the answer is a resounding yes, then adjust your original plan to adopt the new lessons and try again. We all get knocked down, but it is your choice whether or not you want to get back up again.

On the other hand, there are times when ventures just feel right, as if destiny were leading you. Like love at first sight, people have a gut-instinct when a smart business plan and the right timing for it come together. The writing of this book is an example of synergistic events that occurred by living in sync with a higher purpose. After years of planning, tracking case studies, and gathering testimonials from clients, I felt I was ready to write about some of the insights I had gained from meeting so many people. But I recognized that although I knew the content of my book better than anyone else's book, writing was not my forte. After a disappointing false start with a hired writer, I wondered whether the book was as valuable a tool as I had first thought. My determination to put these lessons into print for others to learn from began to waver.

That was when the robin started his assault. As described in the introduction to this book, nothing I did seemed to deter the bird. After tolerating weeks of its bizarre behavior, I began to wonder whether the robin was some sort of messenger pushing me to continue to work on my book in spite of the earlier disappointments. The timing was right, but perhaps I was focused on the book to the point that I was banging my head against the wall with the frustration of planning and gathering case histories to include in the project. I finally handed the book over to a higher power, asking for guidance and the wisdom to let go of this dream if it was not meant to be. Suddenly, out of the blue, another writer literally walked into my life. By taking a step back, releasing my own expectations and emotional ties to my dream, I allowed the natural flow of energy to pour back into the project. This book is the result of that decision and sharing these lessons has brought many unforeseen blessings into my life. Sometimes a wall really is just a window.

Whether your particular wall is an all-consuming project, an addiction, money challenges, relationship issues, family secrets or just plain old sour grapes negativity, these are all hard enough walls to knock the wind out of you. Why keep banging into that wall? Why not recognize it as a window, open it and go through it?

Maybe the robin banging into my window was an illustration of my need to release my own negative patterns around control or to trust a higher power. Maybe he was just a cosmic messenger sent to reaffirm my own belief in writing this book. You can view this book as a robin that has been sent to bang on your window, to wake you up and make you realize that there are some walls you need to turn away from so you will finally say, "You know, I am really tired of banging my head against this wall. I think I will find a different path." My hope is that this book will help you to distinguish walls from windows and guide you on the decisions you make and their consequences. Perhaps reading this book can save you many mistakes in judgment and show you ways to open the windows of opportunity in your life.

There is a saying that luck is when preparation meets opportunity; it is only the preparation component that we have control over. When you live your life with intention, setting goals and remaining open to what life has to offer you, then you prepare yourself to receive. Positive thinking is important but even more important is the action you take. You have to keep taking steps toward a life that you design. Remember that you will stumble, maybe even fall, but get up and carry on. Results take time and effort to achieve. One of my clients volunteered at his local fire department for eight years before he was offered a full-time position; eight years of perseverance resulted in fulfillment of his life dream. Do you think it was worth it? Did he? Absolutely!

I believe if you are living in accordance with your life purpose, then the universe opens up and provides for you. People will come into your life at just the right time; connections will be made and coincidences will occur so that things fall into place and life will feel right. Even the money you need will be there if it is meant to be. When you combine positive energy with your true desires, you will flow freely with the river of life.

Four

Choices in Love

But now faith, hope, love, abide these three;
but the greatest of these is love.

1 Corinthians 13:13

As I shared in the introduction to this book, my work as a psychic does not provide me with any sort of immunity to the universal human experiences of loss, failure, indecision or errors in judgment. My decision to share my insights with a wider audience comes from a place of empathy and true compassion. The root of the word compassion dates back to fourth-century Latin; it comes from two words meaning "together" and "to suffer." I believe this word precisely describes my perspective, for I have also had to learn from my own life lessons, both negative and positive. I have experienced first-hand the painful lessons that I see repeated over and over in the lives of the people who come to me for insight and advice. I am not an infallible oracle. I read what I see in front of me and my gift is the ability to see more than most people—and not just *see* as in psychic ability.

I offer my clients the benefit of observation in case after case of the constant repetition of the same mistakes, the same poor choices and the same outcomes.

My marital history has had its challenges, disappointments and joys. I have been married three times, and I am happy to say that my third marriage is the joyful partnership I always wished for. Ironically, I failed to pick up on the deception in the auras of my first two husbands until it was too late. I have said it before and I repeat: *Never underestimate the power of denial.*

My parents have been married for over forty years. My father is the traditional Italian patriarch. As the eldest of three children, all daughters, I was the first to significantly challenge my father's authority. In my twenties I went on a holiday to Mexico. I met and fell in love—of course, I recognize now that it was the other L-word—with a very attractive Latin entertainer. We eloped within months of our first meeting. Needless to say, the root of my choice to elope was rebellion, though of course it was many years before I could see the truth of that decision.

In hindsight it is so easy for me to read all the warning signs, but it took another betrayal and failed marriage before I really got the lesson. Working through my feelings of failure and humiliation—why did I not see it coming!—provided opportunities for personal growth and learning that I do not believe would have come to me in any other way. By learning from my own painful mistakes, I have been able to interpret the signs I see in others with a clarity that I did not possess at the age of eighteen. Thus, I have not only grown in the practice of my profession through honing my natural abilities, but I have applied my personal lessons to bring good out of experiences that, at the time, I would have gladly avoided.

Pardon Me, But is This the Right Bus?

Here is something I tell my clients when they consult me about unhealthy relationships that are a complete waste of time. "Romances are like buses. If you find you are on a bus that is going in the wrong direction, get off! There will *always* be another bus." Find the relationship that is moving in a direction that is healthy and compatible with your needs, goals and desires.

For those who say that they fear the loneliness that comes with being alone, I say, "Would you rather be on a bus—*any* bus—going in the wrong direction, or waiting for the bus that will get you to the right destination? While you are squirming in your seat on the wrong bus, feeling anxious about the route, you may be missing the bus that was meant for you." Taking the analogy a step further, wouldn't it be better to stop, assess, get off the wrong bus and wait for the right one? While you are waiting you could catch up on phone calls or texting with friends, read that book you were always curious about, master a new skill, help a handicapped or elderly person with their parcels, or study course material on a subject that had always intrigued you. Before you know it, you will have stopped looking for the bus—and suddenly, it will arrive on your doorstep. You may even hear yourself say, "Wait a minute. I don't think I'm ready yet—just let me finish this great book!"

I would love to say that in most readings I see evidence of happy, healthy relationships. Unfortunately, the opposite is true. Over and over again, I see the same problems and patterns repeated by intelligent, otherwise sensible people. In fact, the cycle set in motion by poor decision-making is so repetitive that if I were to lose my psychic abilities tomorrow, I would still be able to accurately predict the outcome of most troubled relationships. All I need to do is listen to how a person speaks about their partner to know if their relationship is built to last or is headed down a rocky road of resentment, deception and division.

As with other key factors about a person's character, history, and current circumstances, information about relationships is communicated to me through auras and tarot images as I proceed through a client's reading. While auras provide significant details about the nature of the relationship and the client's attitude toward their partner, tarot images help to define the character of the partner and how they feel about the client and the relationship. Other images from the tarot fill in additional information about the dynamics of the relationship, including its strengths and weaknesses. I will repeat my earlier warning: my interpretation of the tarot images does not come from classic training. If a reading with a traditionally trained reader of the tarot reveals these cards, do not get confused. In an actual reading, I rely also on psychometry and auras to inform the meaning behind the tarot blocks.

If I see the Two of Clubs or Four of Clubs in a relationship reading, it tells me that anger, resentment and emotional scarring are present. For control issues in a relationship, the Devil image is the key: if the Devil appears right side up beside the image that represents the client in the relationship, then he/she is in control. If the Devil appears in a reversed position next to the client card, then he/she is being controlled by their partner. Often, the Hanged Man makes an appearance in a relationship spread; this block indicates a feeling of being stuck or trapped by circumstances. This may apply to one or both partners.

Even before I begin to read the tarot, the client's aura has told me much about their key relationship issues. For instance, when the aura is dark red and agitated, the message is loud and clear that significant issues exist in their primary relationship.

You don't have to be a psychic to recognize good and bad relationships. How many times have you had a good friend cry on your shoulder about a break-up that you saw coming from miles away? On the other hand, how many times have you found yourself envious of the couple who seems to have the perfect relationship? But what defines a good relationship?

We all have different desires and criteria when it comes to romance and relationship. Some are commonly held values such as trust, honesty, and loyalty; others are very specific, such as whether someone shares particular hobbies or sports; there are even extreme reactions to undesirable traits, like the woman who leaves her husband because his snoring is too loud. Aside from individual preferences, however, we are all the same deep down in our need and desire for companionship; it is in our nature as humans to want to love and be loved. Rooted in our biology, this impulse for partnership is so strong that it can obscure logic, reason and even self-preservation. The information I am about to share has been gleaned through my observations as a psychic, confidante and friend, as well as my own relationships and an arduous personal journey that has taught me the importance of mutual respect, which is founded upon self-respect.

THE CRUX OF A GOOD RELATIONSHIP:
A HEALTHY BALANCE OF POWER

To give context to the meaning of relationship in our modern lives, we need to understand its roots in the development of the human species. Partnership in the time of our *Homo sapiens* ancestors was an absolute necessity for survival. While the female of the species performed the key function of childbearing, she also had a duty to support food gathering activities. In return for her unique childbearing abilities, the male acted as hunter and protector, thus ensuring the safety and survival of the female and her offspring. All of these activities describe a wonderfully designed interdependence between male and female, requiring strategies and underlying agreements in order for the relationship—and therefore the species—to succeed. The basic principle at work in these primitive male/female relationships was that of alliance. Going back to our dictionary definitions, the word alliance comes from the French verb *alier*, meaning, "to combine." Historically, the word was used to refer to a union of marriage, although in more recent history it has adopted some political overtones. In its essence, an alliance is a relationship that describes a merging of efforts for a mutual benefit, one that is balanced and advantageous to both parties. In an ideal alliance, power is evenly balanced, with no party seeking or holding a greater degree of control over the other.

Regardless of underlying issues and motivations, this is exactly what most people ultimately seek in a love relationship. Relationships that reflect the alliance model are represented in the tarot blocks as the Devil on the side of the block, suggesting that control of the relationship is evenly balanced between both partners. When control is not equally distributed, one party's needs are sacrificed to serve the needs or desires of the other. The degree to which this inequality exists determines the level of dependency of the less powerful partner upon the other. In some dependency-based relationships, the locus of control shifts from one partner to another without ever sustaining an equal distribution of power that lasts long enough to get the relationship on track.

When a high degree of inequality exists in a relationship, it can no longer be described as an alliance; at this stage, it is a relationship based on dependency. In a relationship founded on dependency, the lack of self-sufficiency and self-confidence of the less powerful individual leads to a reliance on the other for satisfaction, happiness or even survival. Short of extreme cases which may manifest as severely disturbed relationships, a dependent relationship suspends both partners in a constant state of disequilibrium. The relationship is subject to tension and disagreement, often devolving into a never-ending cycle of argument and reconciliation. This describes a dysfunctional relationship: it cannot function in a wholesome manner under the weight of unequal distribution of power. In order to transform this relationship into a sustainable, healthy and equal partnership, one or both partners must relinquish a degree of personal power.

This model of relationships based on alliance versus dependency is too simple to adequately describe the complexities of human partnerships. Romantic interactions are multi-faceted and are subject to individual motivations, desires and needs based on character traits, experiences, events and circumstances. However, in the chapter that follows, these two definitions will serve to illustrate the differences between a healthy and an unhealthy relationship. We will also examine some of the most common relationship concerns and frustrations, and constructive ways to deal with them in order to put you on the road to securing and ensuring an alliance relationship.

THE TROUBLE WITH WOMEN

While no two relationships are identical, in my work, I have witnessed patterns of behavior that typify troubled unions: unrealistic expectations, change initiated by one partner, and/ or failure to recognize and own a shared responsibility for the problems that exist. No particular behavior or character trait is the sole preserve of one sex or the other; however, I have observed a greater percentage of women or men falling into certain habits. In each of the sections that follow, I hope to share some of the typical behaviors and pitfalls that I see each of the sexes fall into most often.

So many of the women who come to me for advice feel confident in every aspect of their lives except one—they are completely at a loss when it comes to finding, establishing and keeping hold of healthy romantic relationships. I am not picking on women here, but I am sensitive to the unique challenges—and shortcomings— facing the empowered women of today's generation. We have more control over our choices and destinies: no longer are we valued for our child bearing abilities alone; we are doing it all with our own unique style.

In many of the readings I do for successful single women, the Judgment card appears. This is generally an indication of someone who has extremely high expectations of herself to the point where she is seldom satisfied with her own accomplishments. This habitual self-criticism is usually paired with redness in the aura around the third chakra, or upper digestive tract. Stomach problems are often identified as a health issue. The third chakra is the centre of self-worth. Though these women are modern-day champions, handling daily dilemmas with ease and ability, the deep insecurities plaguing their love lives reveals the surprising truth.

This type of woman may be quick to assert that she enjoys independence in her relationship; however, she feels there is an unfair burden of household responsibility expected by her partner. She resents this unequal distribution of chores, such as cooking, housecleaning and running errands but "someone has to do it." Discussions with her partner have usually ended with unfulfilled promises. Time and again, she finds herself picking up clothes at the dry cleaner, buying groceries, planning and preparing meals and taking most of the responsibility for housecleaning. Her unvoiced—or unheard—resentment has begun to creep into their sex life, and with anger quietly bubbling beneath a calm surface it is no surprise that the intimacy she and her partner once shared is fading.

This woman would be shocked to hear me describe her personality as *dependent.* Contrary to what many people believe, a dependent personality is not always marked by financial or overtly emotional reliance on a partner. Often, the more dependent person in a relationship is the one who appears to be in control; their need for approval leads them to accept responsibility for most of the practical and emotional duties required to keep the relationship afloat. The most telling characteristic of a dependent personality is the overwhelming desire to please others, often at all costs. People with dependent personalities base their behavior in relationships upon a deep need for approval from their partner, which may lead them to shoulder far more than their fair share.

At the start of a relationship, one or both partners are often so eager to become the object of the other's affections that no inconvenience or sacrifice seems too difficult to bear gracefully, even cheerfully. People commonly find themselves participating in hobbies, sports interests or cultural pursuits that are not to their taste simply to enjoy being in the company of their new love. How many times have you found yourself doing things that your partner enjoys which are not of your choosing: watching sports for hours at a time, cooking gourmet meals, poking around junk shops, or listening to hard rock or opera; if these are not the sort of activities you generally enjoy, they can be fun at first. You may even see intriguing opportunities to adopt new skills or expertise. However, if you do not develop your own sincere interest in the activity, you may find yourself resenting the time you spend with these pursuits. Unless there is an agreement to spend equal time pursuing interests of your choosing with your partner's willing participation, the erosion of your freedom will become an increasing hardship.

Many women fool themselves into believing that ignoring that small inner voice of discontent serves as proof of their commitment. Even if you believe that your sacrifice is minor and that you harbor no ill feelings over the inequity, the partnership has become imbalanced. Sacrificing your own desires for the sake of pleasing your boyfriend is not guaranteed to win his affections or his gratitude; it may, however, establish expectations that will be difficult or impossible to change as the relationship continues.

The same rule applies to chores and favors. It is a pleasure to show your love by doing special things for your man—a fabulous meal, an unexpected gift or a loving massage at the end of the day are wonderful opportunities to share love and affection. However, unless you are prepared to spend the rest of your days saying, "Can I get you anything else, honey?" don't overdo the maidservant routine.

What if cooking is your passion, you ask. You may take so much pleasure in cooking for your new partner that their enjoyment of the meals you lovingly prepare is enough reciprocation. Be careful! Even if your greatest pleasure comes from whipping up a gourmet spread, if your new partner has never offered to clean up the kitchen afterwards, or has not returned your generosity in some other appropriate way, then you are setting yourself and your partner up for unfair expectations. By taking on an unfair burden of responsibility you not only indicate a willingness to adopt this as a permanent and normal state of affairs, you allow your partner to accept your generosity without offering anything in return. This does not promote equality in a relationship, but instead, sends a message that an unfair division of labor is acceptable.

In time, the occasional twinge of resentment you feel as you scrub pots all alone after cooking a lavish meal will develop into bitterness at not being appreciated. If this happens, then you are probably right—you are being taken for granted, but who is really to blame? Did you not set your partner up to have this sort of expectation? Is your partner at fault if, after years of tolerating an unfair division of labor, you suddenly realize that you have shouldered most of the work while your partner has enjoyed a life of leisure?

If you are one for whom the passionate throes of a new relationship have faded, you may think that all your relationship needs is a spark to rekindle the romance of earlier days. But reviving romantic feelings that once masked your boyfriend's/ husband's annoying habits or faults will not solve the issues in a relationship founded upon inequality. Instead of simply seeking to change his behavior you must also recognize your own part in creating the problems that plague your relationship. Before you can undo the damage and rebuild, it is crucial that you share responsibility for the false expectations that you helped to instill. Your partner is not suddenly taking you for granted, nor has he recently adopted bad habits. The truth is, neither of you is in the "best behavior" stage of the relationship. However, if you are the only one trying to change the status quo, then you had better be ready to shoulder the blame for damage to, or even complete disintegration of the relationship. You are the one who has decided to change the rules.

Not surprisingly, the men who find themselves in relationships with women who describe these circumstances cannot understand what has occurred to cause their partner's sudden dissatisfaction. Their own behavior has not changed. Such a man might wonder what has happened to the woman he fell in love with—when, how and why did that generous, loving, excellent cook of a woman suddenly disappear. She has pulled away, cut herself off from him emotionally and physically. Her rejection, constant disapproval and obvious disappointment wear him down; eventually he becomes angry and withdrawn. The moral to this cautionary tale is to make sure that you are not building your relationship on false promises, whether or not they are spoken. An *I-don't-*

mind attitude that is subject to change—because it simply isn't true—cannot be the basis for a successful relationship. Don't make commitments, in words or in actions, that you don't really mean. If your potential partner has habits that you dislike in the beginning of the relationship, then you really need to ask yourself whether or not you can live with these for a lifetime. The bad habits are not likely to change. If you change your disposition from "I don't mind" to "I can't stand it" a little farther down the road, then you are guilty of false advertising.

There is another very important way that some women set up false expectations, and that has to do with sex. Again, it is not my intention to pick on women or to lay an unfair burden of blame on my own sex. My objective is to share, honestly and without judgment, the insights I have gained from years of discussing the intimate details of men's and women's relationship issues.

In the case of sex, it is my observation that in nearly every case, sexual relations between a man and a woman are initiated by the woman. She is almost always the party controlling whether or when the two will have sex. Beyond a purely sexual one-time encounter, a woman's consent to have sex is motivated by more than a desire for physical satisfaction. If she has dated the man several times then her permission for an increased level of intimacy is at least partly intended to ensure that the relationship continues. By upping the stakes in this way, she hopes to encourage and keep his interest, possibly even enter into a long-term relationship.

This is a dynamic I have observed over and over, and by itself, it is not a cause of relationship issues. The issues arise later in the relationship when the woman's sexual desire for her partner has abated. There are many possible reasons for such a change: a baby creates new demands; career responsibilities or emotional issues take center stage; health problems arise; or a power struggle between the partners is dealt with unfairly with sex used as a bargaining chip. The latter is obviously the tip of an iceberg of complex issues. Whatever the reason, the change in a woman's sexual interest in her partner is likely to leave him perplexed, rejected, frustrated and angry. If it continues for some time without the partners seeking to understand and resolve the underlying problems, the man might even seek out a new sexual partner. The relationship begins to unravel.

Though both partners in such a relationship breakdown bear the responsibility for its demise, this unhappy situation could have been avoided. Women who take the initiative in embarking on a sexual relationship (again, in my experience, this is most women) must understand that their decision to do so has long-lasting implications. Because they chose sex as a means of maintaining their man's interest, they must shoulder the bulk of responsibility for the fall-out that occurs when they suddenly turn the tables.

One of the observations I have made over many years of counseling clients may surprise you. In my practice, I have learned that most people who engage in extramarital affairs do not really want to cheat on their spouses. Though there is a segment of the population who feel compelled to deceive others, this is a very small percentage. In the majority of cases I have seen, people do not really want to cheat on their spouses. After years of a sexless marriage, poor communication, or unresolved resentments they may succumb to boredom or to feelings of not being wanted or desired by their spouse. Most people that I have worked with do not seek out an affair as a preferred option.

Show your spouse appreciation, discuss any disagreements or issues as soon as they arise, and do not take your partner for granted sexually. Rekindling the passion you felt in the beginning of the relationship is a far better choice than looking outside your marriage for replacement partners.

An alliance relationship starts as a partnership between equals. There is no place in such a union for false promises or hidden agendas. If you are seeking a sincere, lasting partnership you must adhere to the basic "truth in advertising" rules. By following this one simple instruction, you can avoid the bad relationship pattern altogether: simply be who you are and what you are from the beginning of your relationship with a potential partner. By the same token, look at the goods on offer with open eyes and not rose-colored glasses. Your willingness to be honest with a potential partner must also apply to honesty with yourself.

THE TROUBLE WITH MEN

To all the men out there struggling to understand the ever-changing maze of male/female relations, I feel your frustration. Previous generations have had the benefit of an unwritten manual of masculinity which has been rendered obsolete. For the first time in the history of human relationships, women are expecting equal partnerships. This means you not only have to show up, you also have to participate. And yet it seems as though the moment you begin to feel comfortable in a relationship, your wife or girlfriend turns the tables on you; suddenly you can do nothing right. The more you do to improve the situation, the worse you feel. You help more around the house than your father ever did and yet it seems you get no credit for it. Not only that, you are constantly faced with reminders that women don't really need you. No wonder you experience so much confusion, insecurity and lack of respect in your intimate relationships. But while I am sympathetic to your situation, I am also frustrated by the way many men flounder in a prolonged adolescent state rather than dealing honestly with the issues underlying this state of dysfunction.

The most common complaint I hear from women is the unfairness of the division of labor between couples and the fact that it can persist in today's modern world. Women are out in the working world achieving all the same goals that men do, but at home, they still seem to be left with the lion's share of household duties. But in spite of the fact that women seem to do more at home than men, what most women really want is some appreciation for their efforts.

Appreciation is not the same as gratitude; it is the recognition and understanding of the real value of someone's time and willingness to act. The only way to truly appreciate the value of someone else's actions is to spend some time doing the same thing yourself. Just what does it take to do umpteen loads of laundry a year, cook hundreds of meals, keep a house clean and tidy or perform the myriad of other day-to-day chores that are part of life? Open your eyes and have a good look around you. Have you really done your share of countless, thankless, mundane tasks? How often lately have you gone around the house to pick up after yourself or your children, do the dishes, or take over parental duties while your wife spends precious time doing something she really enjoys? All of these things are part and parcel of an alliance model between equals. If you do not step up to the plate and do your share, then eventually resentment will build between you and your spouse. One day you will wake up to realize that you have an unhappy partner and you know what that means: *If momma ain't happy, ain't nobody happy.* You will have a woman who is constantly disappointed in you, is never satisfied with anything you do until suddenly an avalanche of resentment descends upon you.

Of course, there are certainly men who still wish for the old days when women didn't seek or demand anything from them apart from a roof over their heads, bread on the table and a safe haven for them and their children. There is no need to feel sorry for those men who don't like the idea of equality. There are plenty of women out there who will dish up absolute servility in exchange for security, but even dependent relationships come at a cost. The roles of such unions are rigid and resistant to change and the weight of having sole responsibility for the happiness of another is a huge cross to bear.

Remember the client in chapter two who turned up the Chariot card? He was faced with a life-altering decision between choosing his lover with whom he had a sizzling sex life, and his wife, whom he still loved and with whom he had built a home and family. Could he reclaim the passion he once felt for his wife and would he feel satisfied? My advice? Why *not*! If you married someone for love, then you probably still love them and the passion can be awakened. You're just bored, or you feel the weight of other pressures such as career, finances, family life, which do not play a part—yet—in your new relationship. Don't blame your marriage for the frustration you feel in these other areas of your life. Those frustrations are yours and yours alone, and they will follow you. If you look at it another way, why are you being so selfish? You are providing sex for this new lover, why not for your spouse?

Don't make the wrong choice out of mere laziness, selfishness or a foolish belief that the grass really is greener over there.

Men who consult me for relationship advice often demonstrate the same level of insecurity as women, but it is manifested in different ways. Whereas insecure women tend to become pleasers, insecure men resort to exerting absolute control; both of these tactics stem from the anxiety of losing their partner. This is usually indicated in a reading by the block showing the Devil, symbolizing control, control, *control*.

While it is true that this theory is a generalization, the fact is that men are genetically hard-wired to protect territory. They are predisposed to the fear of being usurped by another male, a conqueror—some young buck. This innate fear plays out in attempts to control things like wardrobe choices, time limits on nights out with the girls or approval of a partner's choice of friends. In extreme cases, the need for control in a relationship can escalate into violence and abuse; a relationship where abuse is taking place is guaranteed to be rooted in dependence. Recognizing the fear-based origin of control issues is the key to understanding the motivation behind tactics and behavior designed to control others. An approach which acknowledges this instinctual fear while asserting autonomy in making choices helps to build trust and instills a healthy sense of respect between the partners. Resorting to equally destructive methods to avoid being controlled, such as lying and manipulation, only serves to destroy trust, making the situation worse for both parties.

Alliance relationships are based on trust and mutual respect. This creates a climate where free and open dialogue is encouraged and nurtured; in such a relationship, feelings of vulnerability can be claimed, understood and dealt with in positive ways before they manifest into fear-based control struggles.

CONTROL DOES NOT EQUAL CARE

When control issues dominate a relationship the tarot often shows me swords and clubs together. The aura of a person seized by the need to control shows a lot of emotional stress, indicated in very specific areas by the color red. Control issues are not, of course, the sole burden of men. Women can most certainly exhibit severe controlling behaviors, though the two genders show it in different ways.

Often, when women take control in a relationship they believe they are motivated by love. However, their motivation is no different than that of men. The root of their problem is also fear. But they have convinced themselves that their actions are not ways of controlling the relationship; they believe that their behavior is the way that they show their love. In truth, it is simply a way to try to hold onto other people. When women are obsessed with control, their auras show a lot of red around their chest and jaw areas. They grind their teeth at night because they are holding onto the stress and anxiety of what they think will happen if they relinquish control. What will happen if they are no longer needed? Their greatest fear is that their loss of control will amount to losing the love of those they are controlling.

Men who control show red in the area around their backs and necks, which can be taken quite literally to mean they are carrying the weight of the world. They may feel that there is so much pressure on them to provide, to perform, to look after things; they think that asking for help will be seen as weakness.

A Psychic's Guide to A Better Life ☀ 101

Instead of sharing the burden of responsibility, they hold in their anxiety until it manifests in destructive ways such as holding all the purse strings, or making all the significant decisions in the partnership, such as where they will live, or whether or not their wife should work outside the home.

Both men and women who are controllers can let their need to control poison other relationships, besides the primary spousal one. We all know people who constantly buy their children every toy they see advertised, all the latest electronic gadgets and designer gear, even cars and other extravagant presents. If you ask them why they spoil their kids this way, they will defend their behavior as a way to show their love. But in reality, for many of them it is a form of control. By making sure their children come to rely on them for all the luxuries of life, they keep them dependent and needy. Instead of teaching them skills of independent living and self-sufficiency, they entrap them into lives of overindulgence and irresponsibility. Is this the way to show your children you love them and want what is best for them?

Smothering your children with everything they could possibly wish for prevents them from developing normal attitudes toward setting and achieving goals. By showering them with all the things that money can buy, you deprive them of the opportunity to experience first-hand the tremendous satisfaction that comes from working hard to achieve a goal. Many of these children remain dependent all their lives, unable to determine what they truly want in life. Before they can think about it, they are told what they want—the flashy clothes, the late model sports car, the high-rise condo; in the mind of their controlling parent these are the things they *should* desire.

When these controlling types consult me, and believe me, I see it in the cards and in their auras, they are usually shocked to hear me bluntly tell them, "You need to stop trying to control everyone!" And then I hit them with this one, which usually sends them off the deep end. "You are controlling people because you are needy." When they recover from the shock of cold water in their face, they might ask why I would make such a ridiculous statement. I tell them, "You control people because you think that by controlling them, they will love you. You want to be important to them. You want to feel accepted and so you give your children everything with the false belief that because they rely on you, they love you. That's not love. All you have instilled in them is dependence."

Are you recognizing some of your own behavior traits in this description? Are you asking how you can learn to be less controlling, without losing what you feel is love? The way to become less controlling brings us right back to the lesson of chapter two: what other people think of you is none of your business. Stop obsessing about what others think and concentrate on your own opinion of yourself. Exert a healthy control over your own actions, words, thoughts and what you think of yourself. The way to maintain a healthy balance of control within a relationship is by setting boundaries.

R-E-S-P-E-C-T

It's not just a catchy, classic lyric—it's the truth. The most important factor in bringing an alliance relationship into one's life is respect: you must respect yourself and your partner equally. Self-respect requires that you set boundaries for what you will and will not tolerate, which are different for everyone. Your boundaries are your own to decide upon, communicate and uphold. They may be different than the ideals held by your family, social stature, culture and friends. Failure to set and maintain these boundaries will leave the door open to the tricks shown by the the Devil of the tarot and his power plays. What follows is a description of the three most common *Devil-ish* issues that I see in relationships.

I am sure that we have all heard men comment on other women in front of their own wives or girlfriends. The comments might run from a genuine appreciation of her good looks to a vulgar, "Look at those tits!" The shock is not the fact that these men carry on in this way, it is the reaction—or lack of reaction—by their girlfriends and wives, who simply shrug off the comments as harmless, normal or even entertaining. I guarantee you that a man would not talk that way to (or in front of) a woman he respected. Would his mother tolerate it? This sort of behavior may have become habit; it may have started out innocently with a wink or a comment here or there, but over time it has grown to the magnitude of relinquished power, impossible for a woman to retrieve. The cure for this lies in prevention. If this man's wife had set her boundaries early in the relationship to zero tolerance for this sort of behavior there would have been no deterioration of respect and no resultant humiliation.

Ignoring the comment is not the same as dealing with it. To ignore it is to say to a man, "Your respect doesn't matter enough to me to acknowledge when a boundary has been crossed." When your boundaries have been crossed you don't have to be rude or start an argument. All you need to do is state your position. Look the person straight in the eye and calmly but firmly say that you will not accept that sort of behavior. The bottom line is that if you ignore an opportunity to say what you feel is unacceptable behavior, from your children, a partner, or even a friend or relative, then you will be subjected to exactly what you have tolerated whether you like it or not. If you have set the bar of tolerance too low, get used to the idea that what you think and feel is not important.

One of the worst alliance violations is what I call "the disappearing act." This is when the partner, male or female, becomes uncharacteristically unavailable for unexplained lengthy periods of time. The disappearance can last several hours, a day or even several days. It usually starts with an argument, followed by an angry departure; the disappearing partners leave the scene in a huff, and the partner left behind feels overwhelmed with guilt and anxiety. This type of behavior is not only manipulative and disrespectful but can lead to risky extremes. In a situation like this one, no one needs my psychic ability to see the inevitable outcome. In the words of my no-nonsense grandmother, "What do you think he's doing?" She has the right idea. If he is avoiding your calls, he is probably venting his frustration inappropriately and "getting even" with bad behavior such as gambling, drinking, having an affair, or even engaging in criminal activities.

If this describes behavior that you have experienced in your relationship, then I have only one thing to say: leave. This man doesn't care about you. His behavior proves it. He cares about maintaining power in the relationship. With you unable to reach him—he's not answering his cell phone, even just to let you know that he is safe—you are left feeling hurt, helpless and filled with anxiety. Has he left you for good? Probably not. Has he done something to hurt you or to irrevocably damage the trust in your relationship? Probably. What you need now is not a magic tracking device to find him and beg him to come home. You need enough self-respect to end it before it mutates into a physical or emotional illness. Make no mistake: this is abuse in one of its most hurtful forms. This constant state of alarm sends negative energy streaming through your cells, almost certainly manifesting into a mental, emotional, spiritual or physical blockage on its way to full-blown disease.

The third example of the Devil at work is reserved for all the women with boyfriends who cannot commit. If the man you have been seeing for years is still squeamish about making plans for your future together then you need to face the hard truth: though this man probably has some emotional tie with you, he does not really love you. He will never commit to a lifetime with you and perhaps not with anyone else either. But releasing him and yourself from a tie that will never be secured permanently is the most respectful thing you can do for both of you.

How do you know if he loves you but is simply afraid to commit? If your man was in love he would recognize that having you for a lifetime partner was the best thing that had ever happened to him. He would want to seal the deal quick, before you changed your mind or some other guy came along to steal you away. Don't waste any more time waiting for your boyfriend to say he is ready to marry you. I have included this as one of the top three *don't-do-it* scenarios because I have seen it happen so many times I have literally lost count. Even if it does happen eventually, women in these circumstances are often left with a huge burden of deep-down resentment that never goes away. You don't want to hear yourself saying, "Well, I finally wore him down. To stop my nagging, he married me." That is not the image of self-respect you want to carry through the rest of your life. What about raising a family in a union such as this one? Will a man who had to be nagged to marry you suddenly leap into the role of doting father? Respect yourself enough to walk away from half-way or one-way relationships.

Some people are shocked to hear me advise people to walk away from their partners. The truth is, sometimes people get themselves into a rut. If your relationship has spiraled out of control and your partner has no respect for you, you need to let that person go. Forget about what your family, friends, children, colleagues think about you—just let that partner go. To anyone who needs to get this lesson I say, "Go and rent the movie *Shirley Valentine*." This is a film that goes straight to the heart of what happens when you allow the boundaries around a relationship to go soggy and what can happen when you reclaim your self-respect.

You need to be willing to let go of a partner unless they start to show you the respect that every life partner deserves. If you don't, you are going to spend your life manifesting all the hurt and pain that is inevitable in a relationship where respect is lacking. I keep seeing this in one reading after another, so I know what I am talking about. If you do not have self-respect and the integrity to maintain it, how can you possibly create a healthy, successful relationship? So many relationships fail because one or both partners have lost respect for themselves and for each other.

All of the behaviors described above display an unmitigated disregard for the relationship. If these behaviors are not stopped in their tracks the moment they are identified, then they will simply lead to more serious offenses. You can avoid all of these destructive behaviors by firmly setting your boundaries and identifying them to your partner. Be at peace with yourself, be sure that your self-respect button is set high, and keep it there.

As discussed in chapter 2, the power of choice is the most powerful tool that humans possess. The choices we make dictate the lives that we will create. Our choices may also have a wider impact, affecting the lives of parents, siblings, spouses and most importantly, the children in our lives. Children are the carriers of the future and as such, they have the potential to create or destroy all that exists. If we fail to protect the physical, emotional, and spiritual health of the children in our lives, then we fail the human race. I will discuss this further in the section dealing with relationships that include children from previous unions.

Your First Love—You

Finding and keeping a loving, affirming relationship is unlikely to happen if you are unhappy in your own skin. It has been said by grandmothers for generations and shared in hundreds of self-help manuals in recent decades, but the adage still rings true: first you need to love yourself. That means forgiving yourself, building your self-confidence and rewarding yourself for achievements in setting and maintaining healthy boundaries.

If you are new to relationships and still building self-confidence you must realize that to err is human. One of the key ways in which we learn is through making mistakes. The important thing is how you deal with those mistakes so that the lessons you take away will increase your level of self-confidence. If you say the wrong thing to a friend and then say to yourself, "I am such an idiot!" you need to stop and think. What message are you giving yourself? What if instead you said, "That comment I made to Jen was nasty and I feel small and petty when I think about it. I guess I still have to work on thinking before I speak. Maybe I have some jealousy issues to work on." Let self-talk work *for* you, not *against* you.

Self-help books are full of ways to build self-esteem and self-confidence, but the key is finding the method that feels right. I feel foolish when I stand naked in front of the mirror and tell myself that I look good, but I have friends who have had success with that method. What you do need to do is to be intentional with your goals—think about your success and your goals daily. There are many ways of doing this, such as keeping a journal, compiling and reading a list of your best attributes, meditation or automatic writing, and many others. Just be sure to set aside of little portion of your day to do something life-affirming for yourself.

Learning to love yourself can mean the undoing of a lifetime of negative messages. We all keep a memory box full of bad things that have happened to us, harsh words, cruel actions or humiliations that our mind just won't erase. For some people, the voice of negativity and the deprecation just never seems to turn off. If this describes your state of mind, you need to find a way to deal with these voices and negative self-images or you will never be able to live in a state of self-respect.

A severe lack of self-esteem can be linked to old wounds that are deeply rooted in the psyche. While simple exercises in daily affirmations and other self-help exercises may be helpful, if you experience a high degree of self-doubt and a feeling of neediness in one relationship after another, then the most important step to a healthy, alliance relationship is to be honest with yourself. Take some serious steps toward reclaiming your personal power and do not be embarrassed or ashamed to seek professional help to accomplish your goals of self-empowerment. If you have spent years of your life trying in vain to unravel the negative twists in your self-image, then the time you spend in therapy will never be wasted. One of the hardest but by far the most beneficial things you can do for yourself is to build the self-confidence you need to develop self-sufficiency, resilience and independence.

I am often asked how to best deal with loneliness. This can be especially difficult for people if they have just come out of a long-term relationship. Though I don't have any magic solution, I always tell people to wear or carry a piece of rose quartz to soothe feelings of loneliness. Rose quartz is also good for clearing your aura of old negative energy around love, allowing a healthy welcoming attitude toward love to replace feelings of fear, loss or regret.

One last word on loneliness: it is not necessarily a bad thing. Sometimes being alone can be incredibly liberating, giving you a wide-open invitation to really enjoy your own company.

DATING, DIVORCED AND DATING AGAIN

Remember the cave man and woman partnership I described at the start of this chapter? Even after thousands of years of evolution, humans have not strayed very far from our origins as hunters. Our predatory nature is still prevalent in the wild jungle of dating. Carnivores give chase to strong and healthy creatures;

scavengers who prey on the weak and sickly are not the stuff of alliance relationships. Kings of the jungle are looking for queens, not just a scrap of meat to tide them over. Ask yourself what kind of person you would rather date, a lion or a hyena? How would you like to be treated, as royalty or something to chew on until something better comes along? What separates the weak from the strong? Self-respect. A healthy level of self-respect will enable you to bounce back from just about any disappointment.

Take for example the experience of a heartbreaking romance; we've all had at least one—okay, maybe two or three. Some people would recover from the pain of that heartbreak by pulling in their auras and protecting themselves, while others might dive right into the first new relationship that comes along. Though you don't want to pull in your aura forever, taking the time to reflect on what went wrong with the last one before you jump into another is a healthy step toward self-respect. Failing to do so not only leaves you open to choosing poorly, but the urgency to be in a relationship at all times, rather than face the fear of being alone is an indication that you are suffering from low self-esteem.

People who would rather be with *anyone* than spend time alone are known to go to excessive, sometimes self-destructive lengths to obtain the approval they believe they can only get from outside of themselves. They may convince themselves that their relationships are true partnerships, but in reality they do not have the self-awareness or insight necessary to create healthy alliance relationships. These dependent personality types are like character chameleons, able to change their persona—the face they show to the world—to suit the habits and interests of any new partner. In doing so, they often leave behind the friends, hobbies or causes that had been important in a previous relationship. They believe that this is the way they can fit into any environment, but they seldom find a truly comfortable fit. How can they know what feels right if they have never stopped to think about what does and doesn't suit them?

Neediness is not the sort of character trait that one lists when considering the ideal mate for an alliance relationship. Perhaps you have had an experience where passion, lust or longing has clouded your judgment. You may have wanted to belong to someone so desperately that no sacrifice would have felt too great for the reward of feeling accepted, loved or wanted by that person. But what would have happened in this unbalanced relationship? How could such one-sided longing become a bridge into an alliance relationship?

If you have been finished with a relationship for some time and have taken the wise steps of understanding what went wrong with your failed relationship, perhaps you feel ready to get out there and try again. But take it easy. Why not tone down the intensity of the getting-to-know-you stage. I am not saying that you should play games or try to snare a partner with a false sense of aloofness. What I am suggesting is that you set and respect healthy boundaries right from the start of your foray back into the dating sea. There is no greater turn-off than someone who is obviously in the heat of desperation.

There is a list of forbidden first date comments that goes something like this, "Where do you see this relationship going? (*Can you even use the "r" word to describe a first date?*) Do you still have feelings for your ex? (*Even a yes could mean scary feelings, bad feelings, like the one you're giving him/her right now.*) How much money do you make? (*Check, please!*) Don't become

Inspector Clouseau asking all sorts of probing questions about past relationships and please, *please* do not drown your new date in a flood of details about your past failed romances. A first date is just that—a prolonged handshake. Think of it as a quiet moment away from the rest of the world to find out if you want to learn more about this person and if you want to share more about yourself with them—and if you are both in sync with the outcome of those two questions.

If you do start a relationship with someone that you are keenly interested in, take it easy. If falling in love does happen, let it happen naturally and let it happen to both of you. Don't become obsessive if you have fallen for someone and they have not reciprocated. Being pursued is not an attractive prospect for the object of your affections when they feel like they are being hunted. Don't phone or text them incessantly with messages of devotion, and don't talk about the future too early in the relationship. Remember, this is also your opportunity to find out whether this person is potentially the right one for an alliance partnership with you. If you need to manipulate or push your way into a deeper level of intimacy before they are ready for it, then perhaps they will never feel ready. Saying things like, "I just thought it would be easier if I kept some of my things at your place," while you rearrange the medicine cabinet is a terrifying thought in the mind of a person not ready to commit.

Most importantly don't do, agree with or say things that you don't feel or believe just to gain the favor of your new potential partner. Remember the rules and stick to them: no false advertising, no bait and switch tactics. If you repeat those same mistakes, you'll only end up pulling into the next bus station looking for the one headed in the direction you really want to go. Keep in mind also that even great relationships may have their less perfect moments. If you find an equal partnership that has a solid foundation, don't be discouraged if you can still run into some challenges. Work through them with your new partner and you will both find opportunities to grow. There is no harm in reminding each of other of the boundaries and expectations that have been set from time to time; sometimes we need a little regroup to keep everything on track.

If the relationship breaks down with no way to repair it, then maybe it is time to walk away. But be sure that if you walk away you are able to look each other in the eye and say you gave your partner and the relationship the dignity and respect that it deserved.

I have worked with clients who have ended a relationship but still continued to sleep with their ex-partner. Why? This is a powerless position. If someone breaks up with you, hold your head up, reinforce the message—to *yourself,* "I respect myself," and move on. Yes, you will feel the pain of a heartbreak, you may go over and over every aspect of the relationship trying to put your finger on what you might have done wrong, but leave and learn from the experience. Don't stay stuck in a situation that has no further lessons for you.

One of the greatest gifts of relationship is the chance to learn about ourselves, to gain insight into our own true nature and to develop strength of character. Good relationships help people to grow and change; a partnership needs time, effort and commitment to allow these fruits of love to flourish. Sometimes it even requires a complete breakdown in order to be reconstructed into something strong and permanent. If you do reconcile with your partner at some future date, make sure that you are on an equal footing. Set new boundaries and standards and stick to them.

If your relationship failed in spite of your best efforts, it doesn't mean that you are a failure. Bad relationships have a lot to teach us as well. Once you've had one (or in my case, several) you can certainly recognize a good one when it comes along. Love has knocked me down and spun me around so hard that I completely lost my head and every experience has helped prepare me for the alliance relationship I have now. Love has been a very hard lesson for me to learn, but all those bad relationships helped me build the boundaries and standards for the wonderful alliance I have with my husband. Fifteen years ago I would not have appreciated my husband; I still had hard lessons to learn. We are all at different pit-stops on the journey of love and happiness; some people need more learning experiences while others have identified their relationship needs. Once you know better, you can do better.

If you look at a scale that measures the impact of certain events in your life, I think you might be surprised that the death of a spouse and divorce are not very far apart. When you go through a divorce, no matter how difficult or simple, you still need to give yourself time to grieve the loss of your marriage. There are no hard and fast rules in any grieving process because everyone grieves in their own way; there is no right or wrong way to experience and work through these deep emotions. Once you have travelled through all the steps in the grieving process you will be ready to regroup, evaluate and begin the genuine healing journey.

There are lessons to be learned from the process of divorce.

Don't bury yourself in guilt and blame because that will only push the lesson out of your grasp. You can rise from the ashes stronger than before. Take the time to reflect, revise your boundaries and reinforce your self-respect before you dive back into the dating pool.

THE GOOD STUFF

So if there is so much pain and angst in the mechanisms of love and relationships why do we do it? Easy—the joy of a solid partnership with another person who actually cares about you, shares your dreams, lends a helping hand or reaches out for yours when they need support is without question one of the greatest opportunities in life. It's good for your skin, it's good for your heart and it brings you as close to God as you can get—at least, in this life!

Love in the tarot is symbolized by The Star and by any cards in the cups sign, especially my favorite, The Ace of Cups, which signifies a future of peace, love and fulfillment. Love makes auras glow, not only in the early stages of romance, but even for partners who have been together for years. With their hearts tied in a genuine bond of commitment, they still glow brightly for each other.

Do you feel that disappointments mean that romance and partnership are simply not in your cards? Don't be too sure. Love can change your life in an instant and at any age. I once did a reading for Marion, an 84-year-old woman who fell in love with a boy at school when she was 15. Marion's mother disapproved because he was from the wrong side of the tracks. Succumbing to family pressure, my client married a man her family found more suitable and the two had a long marriage, fulfilled by a home and children, which lasted until his death. Widowed in her late seventies, Marion returned to her hometown to visit old friends. Enter serendipity. During the visit, Marion ran into her long-lost love and was thrilled when the old flame between them was rekindled. In her reading, she confided that, in spite of her happy marriage, she had never felt anything like the joy and romance that her first love brought to her life. If an 84-year-old widow can find romantic bliss then surely, the hope must never die.

If you believe deeply that you are meant to be with a partner, take heart. While I do not have any magic potions or a book of secret love spells to help you in your search for a healthy, life-affirming relationship, I can offer the following advice to guide you toward finding one:

- Pay attention to behavior that signals disrespect and refuse to accept it.

- Don't employ false advertising or bait-and-switch tactics. Be true to yourself and about yourself right from the start.

- Respect yourself enough to walk away when your standards are compromised.

- Make sure your actions and words are in alignment with your beliefs.

- Respect what your potential partner brings to the relationship.

- Reflect on bad relationship experiences and learn from them.

- Make your goal an alliance relationship and expect the love you deserve.

Five

The Grey Veil of Drug Addiction

And do not lead us into temptation, but deliver us from evil
Matthew 6:13

Drug abuse is a dirty little secret. Unfortunately, I witness this common secret in a lot of readings. Drug users come from all walks of society. I see mildly sedated mothers, coked-up businessmen, the elderly addicted to prescription painkillers, kids and adults on oxycodone; all of these are the various faces of addiction that have become commonplace. But common as it is, drug addiction is terrifying; its widespread use and the new generation of drugs that is on the rise in all social circles make it the number one social ill of our time.

Drug abuse changes you, your aura and your soul. There are no surprise outcomes of drug abuse; failures in all cornerstones of life are very predictable: relationships, health, career and family are inevitable. So why do people engage in drug abuse? It most often begins in what seems a bit of harmless recreation. But my experience in working with addicts has shown me that experimentation with drugs often escalates quickly. Drug use leads to a diminishing of a person's natural inhibitions, but not in the sense we usually mean when we speak of a loss of inhibitions; there is a loss of spiritual essence, or more accurately, there is a very great danger that one's spiritual essence will be drained. I will explain what I mean by this statement.

When you fall under the influence of drugs designed to give feelings of euphoria, your spiritual compass gets bypassed—drug abusers experience a loss of morals which in the addict becomes a complete disregard for anything except maintaining their high. I have seen this manifested in the auras of drug users; drugs have a very strange and visible effect on auras. Instead of a retracted aura like that of abused and emotionally scarred people, the aura of a drug user presents itself as wide open, with no self-protection or barrier against negative influences. When an individual's aura is left wide open like this, with no moral buffer zone, the individual becomes a magnet for invading entities that I referred to earlier as *the greys*. These entities are parasites that attach themselves to the auras of individuals who have left themselves vulnerable. The intent of the greys is to bolster their own energetic frequencies by feeding of the energy of unsuspecting victims. They are literally energy vampires.

If this sounds like a plot line from a horror movie, let me assure you that it is exactly like a horror movie. I see the greys as thin grey wisps that are attached to auras of addicts. They live by draining energy from the auras of unwary people, with the result that their victims become increasingly fearful, angry, resentful, and unmotivated to change or improve their lives. The greys will suck all the ambition and appreciation of life out of you. When I see the greys feeding on an aura, I recognize that the individual is unknowingly hosting a parasite. This parasite will eventually lead the individual to lose their sense of truth and morality; this is the reason that so many drug users spend their lives mired in negativity, often ending in tragic consequences.

Id, Ego and Superego

I can describe drug abuse in another way. Sigmund Freud developed a theory of the three functions of the mind, represented by the id, the ego and the superego. The following is a simplistic explanation of how these three functions of the mind work together. Id is simple, amoral and seeks instant gratification. Id controls primal needs like food and functions such as sex and aggression. Now enter ego. Ego is the rational, organized and logical voice of the mind whose job is to keep the id in check so that it does not run rampant. Ego, in turn, is kept in line by superego, which lets the ego know when it has failed to control the id. How does the superego accomplish this? As the internalized authoritarian, superego unleashes feelings of remorse, guilt, shame and humiliation onto the ego when the id is permitted to get out of control. However, the superego cannot communicate directly with the id, making the ego the essential link between human conscience and animal instinct within the mind of an individual.

A visual of this mental dynamic might look something like this: id is a horse—a creature of innate sensibilities; ego is the horse's rider. As the rider, ego is responsible for navigating the horse, controlling its direction, speed and movements. Now let's add drugs or alcohol to the picture. Drugs and alcohol go directly to the creature brain, and all reason flies out the window. In this imaginary scenario this would look like the rider (ego) getting thrown off the horse. Once the drugs take hold of the id, it becomes focused solely on getting more of the stimulation that resulted in momentary pleasure. Without a rider to control it, the released id indulges all its primal desires: sex without conscience, possession (theft and crime) and violence (to obtain and keep possessions). Without a guiding sense of morality, the primal creature part of the mind is not aware of or concerned with the consequences of its actions. In this example, addiction has rid itself of ego and with it the pathway to superego so that all sense of responsibility, guilt, remorse and shame are left lying in the dust. When I look into the eyes of these horses without riders, I am frightened by what I see: they are vacant, and no one is in there controlling their actions. Severe addicts have the look, feel and presence of zombies; seeing them sends shivers down my spine. Not only are they physically empty but also spiritually, their energy having been sapped by the eerie grey veils of addiction. Yes, it truly is a horror story, but unfortunately it is real.

I do not need more confirmation of affliction than what I see in the auras of addicted individuals, but if I did, the tarot blocks confirm that these people are under dangerous assault by the greys. In the tarot blocks drug addiction is indicated by the Hanged Man or the Devil reversed, both of which represent loss of personal control. Another common thread in readings for addicts is the indication of loss of money, represented by the clubs appearing above the coins. In the early stages of drug abuse,

I often see also the Judgement block reversed and next to many clubs, which shows me that the individual suffers from feelings of shame.

Here is the most important wake-up call for people playing with fire—using drugs to get high. It might help if more people are aware of the possible outcome of their actions before getting tangled in this web of woe. As I see it, there are only four possible outcomes of involvement in drugs:

1. Do drugs once, recognize your mistake and feel thankful to never do them again.

2. Do drugs, get addicted, hit rock bottom and then start the long slow climb to get free.

3. Do drugs, become addicted and die of an overdose or from the many health-threatening consequences of drug addiction.

4. Do drugs, become addicted for the rest of your life (which will inevitably be shortened). You will experience all the worst that this life has to offer including loss of dignity, the love, support and respect of friends and family, and eventually, whatever financial resources, regardless of how wealthy you are to begin with. You may even end up living on the street and resorting to crime to finance your habit. By this time you will have lost everything including your sense of self-worth.

I did a reading for a man I will call Ian who was experiencing some problems in his marriage. Instead of seeking solutions, he avoided confronting the problems and instead began to visit bars and strip clubs on a regular basis. During his outings on the shady side of the street, Ian met a woman with whom he began a physical relationship. In his mind, he thought he was having the most wonderful illicit affair, free of responsibilities. The woman introduced Ian to crack cocaine; he enjoyed the high so much that he became addicted. All this time Ian's perception of his activities was that he was having fun, not hurting anyone and enjoying his escape from his troubled marriage. Before long the crack cocaine wasn't giving him the same thrill. He turned to heroin and crystal meth to crank up the high and suddenly he was a full-blown addict, not thinking of or caring about anything except how he was going to score his next hit.

The woman he had been having an affair with had already moved on, looking for someone new to introduce drugs to who could support her habit. Ian was so addicted he couldn't—and wouldn't—spare any cash or share drugs. His wife had given him an ultimatum: either he seek immediate help for his drug habit, or she would leave him. His employer was tired of excuses for his lack of performance and told him that if he did not enroll in the rehabilitation program offered through his work, he would lose his job.

Remember the split path I talked about in chapter 2? Ian was looking at a just such a split in his path. He could continue on the road he was on and lose his wife, his job and undoubtedly his life, or he could choose the other option of admitting his addiction and seeking rehabilitation. What do you think Ian did? I would love to tell you that he did the right thing, went to rehab and cleaned up his act, but unfortunately he chose to stay on what seemed the easier path and continued the downward spiral of self destruction and despair. Within a year, Ian lost his job, his family and his home. Turning to petty crime he got into trouble and ended up in court, which resulted in a court-order that forced Ian to begin a rehabilitation program.

While Ian was in rehab, he slowly began to realize what he had done to his life. Fortunately for Ian, he rediscovered the person he had once been and began the long arduous journey back from the black hole of emptiness he had chosen. He worked hard to turn his life around; he took responsibility for his actions and cleaned up. He was granted visitation rights to see his children, provided he submitted to and passed the random drug tests. But he still had to rebuild every other part of his life that he had thrown away.

If only Ian could have paused at the critical crossroads in his life to think about the outcome of the path he was choosing— what a different outcome his story would have had. He could have avoided all the suffering inflicted on his family and himself.

This is just one example of what I mean by *don't miss the wake-up call!*

The Tarot blocks of another young man, Jerry, told me a similar tale. Jerry wasn't unhappy or experiencing any major problems in his life when he was invited by a friend to try drugs and get high. At that moment, Jerry was faced with a split path; he could have said no and just continued on his merry way. Instead, he thought about it for a moment, decided there was no harm in trying it and said, "Sure." He didn't think about it too long or too thoroughly did he? After his first experience of getting high, Jerry began to crave a repeat performance. He got high again and again until he found that he could not get enough—it became an obsession. Despite the tell-tale signs, Jerry's parents were in complete denial over their son's drug abuse. But he got into so much debt trying to satisfy his addiction that he had to seek his parents' financial help. His parents were forced with the shameful, terrible fact that their son was a drug addict who was in desperate need of their help. But Jerry's mother still could force herself to face the truth and accepted Jerry's transparent excuses for his financial troubles. Instead of insisting that Jerry seek help for his addiction, she helped pay his debts. She could accept that he was spending his money irresponsibly but she refused to believe that he was a drug addict. In fact, she participated in his denial until the day he died of a drug overdose.

Another reading I did was for Josh, an intelligent, capable young man who had grown up in a prosperous, well-educated family. He had nothing but good prospects for his future! While still a teenager, he indulged his curiosity and started to experiment with drugs. Though his friends and family were aware of Josh's drug-related activities, no one had the courage to face him with the truth. After graduating high school, he declined going to university, secretly planning to earn money as quickly as possible to support his growing habit. Josh wandered through a series of jobs but his poor performance, a direct result of his drug use, meant that one after another employer let him go. Josh was never held accountable by his family; in fact, his family always made excuses on his behalf: it was the company or the people he worked with; it was the economy or an industry slump; or whatever excuse they could come up with but never the cold hard truth that his drug addiction, once detected, was not going to be tolerated by any employer.

This young man had a great opportunity through the family business to become a successful business man; he would have to work hard and long hours but it was his for the asking. However, he had now started to sell drugs on the side, this was easy money compared to working long hard hours. He was now looking at a split path - does he go work for the family business or does he continue down the path of doom and destruction? Again, I wish I could tell you that he made the right decision, but now here again is the path of wrong choice winning (momentarily) again. He was successful as drug dealers go; he made lots of money and bought a big house, fancy car and nice clothes. His addiction got worse and worse to the point that his bad habit was eating into his profits. Now he was getting desperate to keep up the heavy flow of cash and support his habit. Too bad he made another wrong decision to screw over some nasty people. He was forced to sell everything to pay off his dangerous debt. He now finds himself living in his mother's basement. His mother supports him and his drug habit.

I have seen through these readings that there are many levels of addiction, and like drugs, addictions come in an astounding array. The most common addictive substances used by people who come to me for advice are marijuana, cocaine, ecstasy, methamphetamine and oxycodone. From what I have seen of the nature and rapidity with which these drugs take hold and destroy lives, it is my opinion that the two most destructive of the drugs in wide use today are oxycodone and crystal meth. Here is a brief overview—call it "Kim's Narcotics 101."

STREET DRUGS

Street drugs are strictly illegal substances and for that very reason the people in the trade who manufacture, smuggle and sell these substances make a lot of money. According to a United Nations survey reported in 2003, the worldwide value for drug trafficking was at that time exceeded only by the whole of the arms trade, both legal and illegal.[2]

MARIJUANA

Regardless of my political opinions regarding marijuana, which lean toward licensing and heavy taxation, as a psychic I will say unequivocally that pot is not without its damaging side effects; I have seen them. In addition to a habitual pot smoker's chronic lack of motivation, the effect on their aura is subtle but unmistakable. When a marijuana user approaches me, I can see the area around their stomach demonstrates pressure—sometimes their aura looks like it's being squeezed and will show up as dull, very lacking in energy. Prevailing wisdom tells us that smoking pot makes people relax, it mellows our moods, however, in my experience, regular marijuana users—daily, constant users, what I call the "wake and bake" variety—typically experience panic attacks, heart palpitations and vomiting. While smoking pot does not, of itself, leave one open to invasion by the greys, the way hard-core drugs do, too much pot replaces ambition with anxiety. Anyone who falls into regular use of marijuana as a method of managing stress is tragically mistaken and will only cause their feelings of anxiety to deepen. More worrisome, however, is the very real danger that pot smoking often leads to experimentation with harder drugs. And I have already given examples of what experimentation can lead to: addiction, the loss of all that is meaningful in one's life, and even death.

2   Page at http://www2.parl.gc.ca/Content/LOP ResearchPublications/ bp435-e.htm#theinternationaltx

COCAINE AND CRACK

Cocaine and *crack*, the poor man's cocaine, are equal opportunity narcotics with a wide appeal. I have had clients ranging from teenagers to geriatrics, business people to busboys, vegans, truckers, teachers, and health professionals who struggle with cocaine and crack addictions. I can spot a cocaine addict by their nervous energy and the red, agitated glow of their aura. In the early stages of addiction, coke addicts come across as cocky and narcissistic, and usually adamantly deny that they feel any dependence whatsoever on the drug.

Cocaine is obtained from the leaves of the coca plant, and it is extremely psychologically and physically addictive. Frequently, however, addicts are introduced to coke's cheaper cousin from the wrong side of the tracks: crack, which is made by thinning out pure cocaine with baking soda and then smoked in a pipe. An even more dangerous form of crack is made by mixing a salt substitute, ether and cocaine. Crack attracts the greys. Cocaine and crack addictions, without fail, have a serious detrimental effect on an individual's life, including financial and emotional losses, loss of self-respect and all those other wonderful things in life and, oh yes, even loss of life.

ECSTASY

Ecstasy (methylenedioxymethamphetamine or MDMA) is derived from the fruit or bark of the sassafras plant and is usually compacted into pills or made into powders. Use and possession of this drug are criminal offenses in all countries of the world. Originally touted as an aid to marital strife because of its anxiety-reducing properties, ecstasy is in wide use as a recreational drug.

It is known to create feelings of intimacy, euphoria and well-being. It is said to release oxytocin, the natural chemical in the mammalian brain released in women after childbirth or following orgasm (in both sexes). The function of the naturally-occurring hormone is to facilitate bonding and trust between mother and newborn child, or between individuals following sexual intercourse. There are studies that suggest that long-term use of the synthetic version of this hormone will eventually inhibit the body's ability to produce it naturally.

While research on ecstasy remains, at the time of this writing, controversial and inconclusive, I have seen firsthand the long-term effects of ecstasy addiction. Due to the relative newness of the drug and lack of definitive information, many addicts and users take a nonchalant attitude, while suppliers of the drug can get away with the its false reputation for being harmless. This is a drug that alters your brain chemistry, causing a multitude of side effects such as anxiety, memory loss, depression, and permanent uncontrollable eye movements. Inconclusive or not, the evidence is clear: ecstasy is a very dangerous drug. I have witnessed the fact that habitual use of this drug attracts the greys. While the id released from its confines by ecstasy is rarely aggressive, the unbridled id is prone to abandon everything in pursuit of pleasure and more pleasure, sometimes with fatal results.

I had a client about eight years ago who had developed a daily ecstasy habit. When I met him he was only 18 and had already had two near-death experiences related to his use of ecstasy: once, he nearly froze to death from lying in the snow for hours; on another occasion his heart raced uncontrollably (most ecstasy is laced with speed) causing him to collapse in the street. The reading I did for him revealed the split path I have mentioned previously. On one side of the path, I saw images representing shame, financial loss and in the near future, death. The other path led to seeking help and eventually to a career in the field of law enforcement, represented by the image of Justice. As discussed in previous chapters, a split path revealed in a reading indicates a critical turning point where one's choice determines the outcome of rest of one's life. I advised him of the options: confide in a person he could trust, get off drugs with a chance to secure a future in the legal profession, or, continue doing drugs and die within the next year.

With all the people I meet, I often have no knowledge of actual events that later occur in the lives of those who have sought my advice. However, a few months ago I was waiting in line in a bank when a very tall, muscular young man wearing a police uniform approached and asked me if I remembered him. Instantly I knew him, and the split path reading just described came back to me. It was the young man I had done the reading for eight years before, and without having to ask, I knew that he had taken the right path. Seeing him in that uniform, so confident, healthy and handsome was one of the most rewarding and pivotal moments of my life. This confirmation that I had helped a confused young man choose the right path simply by sharing what was hidden from view is one of the factors that motivated me to publish this book. The choices were his alone to make, however, insight into the inevitable outcome of continued drug use helped him to move in the right direction. How many others are out there waiting for the wake-up call that will liberate them?

METHAMPHETAMINE AND CRYSTAL METH

Like most recreational drugs, those in the methamphetamine (meth) family create feelings of euphoria, excitement and temporarily increase energy levels. They are also highly addictive. Because this drug helps users, initially, to maintain alertness and mental clarity it is very prone to abuse.

Today, most street meth is manufactured in home or motel labs employing a cocktail of household cleaning products and over-the-counter allergy medications. Because it is so easy to make labs can operate literally anywhere and it is impossible to find all of them. Meth has particularly nasty side effects including amphetamine psychosis, rapid tooth decay (known as meth mouth), a flesh-crawling sensation associated with picking at the skin, and compulsive sexual behavior.

I have done many readings for young women who have smoked a joint at a party, unaware that it was laced with meth. Within months their lives revolved around the drug. Meth is the single most effective way to age and distort your body; loss of teeth, blistery holes in the skin, and lack of interest in hygiene combined with a scratch-that-itch sexual aggression. It is distressing to see these girls with all the potential of youth literally disfigured in exchange for a short-term high.

Meth seems to be the express train to rock bottom. I have seen meth addicts with completely grey auras, which are usually only seen in people who are very close to death. This death/ meth aura tells me the soul of the person has already been eclipsed and has left the earthly plane. Readings for meth addicts are so dark they actually frighten me. Their grey auras pulsate, the tarot blocks are all negative, and the objects for psychometry relay a profound emptiness. All their energy is focused on how, when and where they will score their next high.

PRESCRIPTION DRUGS

After reading about the abuse and dangers of illegal drugs, you may wonder why I would include a section here on legal or prescription drugs—if a drug has been prescribed by a doctor, how can it be classified dangerous? Are prescription drugs really as potentially dangerous as illegal drugs? The answer is yes, of course they are. Just because a drug falls into the category of legal does not mean that individuals are taking the drug as a treatment for an illness. Though many people need the help of drugs to deal with serious clinically diagnosed physical, emotional, and/or mental conditions, the trade in such drugs amounts to billions of dollars when they are sold for purposes for which they were not intended—to get high. In history, drugs such as caffeine and nicotine have been readily available since they are considered harmless, or at least safe. Though we are now aware of the dangers of even these so-called safe drugs, a much greater danger lies in the abuse of drugs which are legally prescribed for treatment of diagnosed diseases. When taken outside of their intended realm of use, these prescription drugs become every bit as dangerous for their addictive, sedative or mood-altering properties—precisely the same qualities for which they are sought after by addicts.

OXYCODONE

Oxycodone is an extremely addictive opiate designed for the relief of severe pain. It is a prescription drug that makes its way to the streets though faked prescriptions, doctor shopping, and robbery. This drug produces an opiate high, and is sometimes referred to as "hillbilly heroin." Oxycodone is an extended release drug, but users often remove the tablet coating and crush or chop up the tablets, allowing them to ingest the entire dosage. Some of my clients have even told me they liquefy it and inject it into their veins. Oxycodone is another soul-stealing substance. It dulls the addict into paralyzing apathy, attracts the greys, and leaves a trail of hopelessness behind it.

Even if prescribed by a doctor and taken as directed, oxycodone has addictive and destructive potential. I have done many readings for successful men and women whose lives were ruined by oxycodone addiction. My client Larry was a self-employed electrician in southern Ontario. He suffered a back injury while on the job and was prescribed oxycodone for pain relief. Within months, Larry became so addicted to the drug he suffered panic attacks and physical withdrawal within four hours of his last dose. He sold all of his belongings to support his habit, got into debt and lost his company, home, family, and integrity. The last I heard of Larry was that he was homeless, a junkie, and panhandling on the streets of downtown Toronto to support his habit.

One of my clients, Jim, was a respected fire chief; at 64 years old, he was just one year away from retirement with a full pension. He was looking forward to fulfilling a lifelong dream he shared with his wife of traveling by RV across the country. He had always been passionate about music and had planned to perform in small venues along the way. When Jim last consulted me, he was in a terrible state. He had been involved in a car accident and was prescribed oxycodone by his doctor. Surprisingly quickly, he became seriously addicted; he lost interest in music and his desire to travel. Unable to work—no longer because of pain but because of his addiction, he had to rely on disability insurance. He became a changed man. His wife mourns the loss of her husband as though he had died. The last time I saw Jim, the change in his appearance and demeanor stunned me so much I was moved to tears: this man, who less than a year ago thought the best part of his life was just beginning, had turned into a sad old man overnight, slumped in his armchair, defeated and spiritless. Unfortunately my advice to get help with this situation did not work.

In my opinion, oxycodone is being overprescribed. Many of my clients who are addicted to oxycodone are construction workers or other trades-people who suffered work-related injuries. From what I have observed, this is a serious and highly addictive drug.

OTHER DRUGS

I find that most prescription painkillers derived from opiates, such as Percocet, Percodan, and codeine to name a few, attract the greys. The result of addictions to this kind of drug follow the same patterns described as above: apathy, negativity, and loss of interest in life. Other opiates, such as heroin, show similar effects on peoples' auras, revealing dullness, redness and blocks. I haven't had as much experience reading those addicted to heroin as I have with other addicts, however I know from readings with the family members of these lost souls that the heroin path is as predictable and tragic as it is with addiction to other opiates.

ALCOHOL

The repercussions and dangers of alcoholism are just as serious and every bit as prevalent as street and prescription drugs.

Alcohol mainly manifests in the aura as a health issue. I have seen the greys on certain people who drink habitually; they attract the greys because they lose their sense of morality. Some people wake up the day after getting drunk and realize what they have said or done and they feel remorse but sometimes they are too far gone. Alcoholism destroys families, ruins lives, and literally kills people around the world every day.

The auras of heavy drinkers show an overall whole-body sickness; their energy has a parched and dry feeling. Their physical appearance looks subdued, their skin is dull-looking and their veins may look as though they are sitting on top of the skin. Often I see a lot of shame surrounding an alcoholic. It's as though the alcohol releases the id in the same way that drugs do, but there is a residual psychological hangover, as well as the physical one. After indulging in excess, the alcoholic has to face the music when the superego steps in with a big dose of humiliation, shame and self-recrimination. Often a cycle begins where the individual drinks too heavily, acts out, feels guilty and fully of shame, and then self-medicates with alcohol to escape those bad feelings. Added to that is the added kicker of physiological addiction, which manifests in the body in ways that one would think would deter anyone from overindulging. Unfortunately, the memory and resolve of the alcoholic to not get drunk seems to last only as long as the hangover of the moment.

Thanks to the well-known 12-step program developed to help recovering alcoholics, the first step to beating addictions, admitting you have a problem, has become common knowledge. Sometimes in readings I am able to scare people straight; when I tell them point-blank what their future holds if they continue on the path of addiction, they take heed, even if only momentarily. But no matter how powerful my psychic abilities may be, I cannot wave a magic wand or give anyone any smoke-and-mirror tricks for escaping from under the grey veil. If you believe you are addicted to anything, as a psychic I advise you to surround yourself with white light and pray to God or whatever higher power you believe in to help guide you and give you strength every day or every hour depending on how much you need. I also advise you to seek the help of professionals, of self-help and support groups that are available in nearly every community in the western world; many more groups are on the internet. Also, smudging your aura will help to cleanse the negative energies clinging to it; carrying citrine stones will conduct negative energy to one's higher self for purification and transformation. Most importantly, be intentional and know the risks involved in using any drugs or alcohol, whether as a recreational stimulant or treatment for a health condition, before your recreational/medicinal consumption becomes an all-consuming addiction.

Chapter 6

Money Makes People Funny

For what does a man profit to gain
the whole world, and forfeit his soul?
Mark 8:36

To say that my second divorce got a little messy would be an understatement. My ex-husband and I spent months fighting over the division of money and property. All the fighting, blaming and arguing was getting us nowhere until finally we found ourselves in front of a judge one day in a sweltering courtroom in Seminole County. His name was Judge Smith, and he was a real honest-to-goodness southern boy with the molasses drawl to prove it. As he prepared to hand down his ruling after listening to our accusations and recriminations back and forth for some time, the judge slowly shook his head, looked my ex-husband in the eyes and said, "M-y gra-a-nd-daddy Smith used to say, 'Money makes people funny.'" I realized that the judge read right through the situation: MONEY. After all these years, that one comment has stuck with me, and whenever I do readings that show me money as the root of the problem in a person's life, I remember the judge's words.

I now have something to add to Judge Smith's granddaddy's saying: Money doesn't just make people funny, it makes them crazy, stupid, outrageous and most of all, disillusioned! Used unwisely or unfairly money can wield a terrible, fearsome power; it can destroy not only marriages but all kinds of relationships such as those between parent and child, siblings, business associates and friends. Money has the power to make people happy and at the same time, it can just as easily make you feel miserable. And it is not only the lack of money that makes people unhappy. Many people of very modest means or even those with barely enough to sustain life can and do find happiness. Just as many very wealthy people are desperately unhappy because of it, having money is not a guarantee of happiness or personal satisfaction. In this chapter I will examine the nature of the power of money and our covetous culture, which shapes our attitudes about money. I will reveal how money can be used as a destructive or transformative force in personal and business relationships.

In the tarot, money is represented by the image of coins— no surprises there; this in itself underscores the significance of money in our lives. There are varying interpretations of how the coins present themselves. When I see the Six of Coins that suggests an improvement in finances of a raise in pay, the Nine represents comfort and good investment choices. The Ten of Coins is prosperity and wealth and the Ace of Cups is the image of the ultimate golden future. In readings, I rely on combinations to reveal the entire financial picture; for instance, the Tower can mean buying a home or an investment in real estate if next to coins. When the Chariot, with the image of the two horses facing in different directions next to coins indicates a decision about money, something like a contract or an investment, when I see this I interpret it as a careful deliberation being needed. The Wheel of Fortune is generally a lump sum of money which could be a settlement, an inheritance or even a lottery payout. One of the most often asked questions is "Am I going to win the lottery?" I have seen in some readings a sum of money being won, but to everyone, sums of money mean something different. To one person, winning $1,000 could be a huge amount of money, but to another it would be nothing. So what would you consider worthwhile lottery winnings? Is it $1,000 or $10,000 or would it need to be 10 million? Winning the lottery has many different connotations for people. When the Star, giver of life in the tarot, is next to images of coins or the Wheel of Fortune, it means something very fortuitous is going to happen. Financial problems are presented as coins around clubs, which can mean challenges, problems or anger. Also, I see financial problems when the reversed Devil shows which means loss of control, or the Hanged Man which means being powerless and stuck in a less than ideal situation.

As for auras, financial or other stress is usually held in the emotional center of the body, the third chakra, which is located in the solar plexus. A red glow around the digestive organs tells me of inner turmoil caused by financial problems that affect the subject's emotional life, the same way that inner turmoil is seen in the aura of a person in a bad relationship or someone who stays at a job they despise, just for the money.

A Brief History of Money

The history of money as we know it—a token that is merely representative of value—dates to a couple thousand years BCE. Prior to the use of precious metal as a token of value, grain, livestock and other goods were bartered based on agreed measures of the value of each. The only problem with this system was its fundamental requirement: you had to have something that someone else wanted, and it may take several rounds of trading before you achieved the precise article you wanted. Your five bushels of grain may have been worth a trade for a few sacks of salt, however, you may have needed to go through several further trades to achieve the spun yarn or cloth you needed. Eventually, most cultures around the world came up with their own individual form of metal or paper money that could be used to obtain anything.

But the idea of money remains abstract. It is of value only as a symbol. Currency was originally a promise to the bearer that the paper could be redeemed for a material object, usually a unit of precious metal like gold or silver. Though today's money markets are still based on the value of precious minerals, money is more often moved as numbers on an electronically exchanged balance sheet. With more prevalent use of credit and debit cards, on-line banking and even coffee cards around the world, the need and use for actual cash becomes less and less. As individuals, we are becoming farther removed from the global flow of finance. Money we used to hold in our hands has become a less tangible, sometimes invisible phenomenon, imbuing it with an almost surreal power. Given its universal use to obtain everything from food and shelter to rocket rides, money has taken on such huge proportions that in its shadow, the individual cannot help but feel small and powerless.

COVETOUS CULTURE

Money is not at the root of all of life's problems however, one of money's ugliest attributes is its power to bring out the worst in human nature. During my years of readings I have seen the destruction that money has wrought in families and relationships of all kinds. Friendships, marriages and blood ties have all fallen victim to the abuse of money. Greed, envy, lust, apathy, pride— five of mankind's greatest weaknesses can surface by the abuse of money, or more correctly, the abuse of the power of money.

For some people there never seems to be enough money. How much money does any one individual really need? Some are so driven to acquire more and more money that they lose sight of most important quality we possess as humans: the ability to love and care for another. It is our compassion, the ability to care for another (whether human or animal), our readiness to reach out to someone in need, and our acceptance and willingness to need others that truly defines us as superior beings.

Beyond maintaining a basic existence, the craving for money has become another drug. It is no longer enough to have food, shelter and comfort. Most of us have experienced the sense of competition that accompanies success, even minimal success. Instead of feeling pleased and content with our homes, cars, clothes and amusements, we constantly look over at our neighbors' pile of goods. Is their pile bigger and better? Does it make us less than them if our pile is more humble? What is the incessant drive to not only "keep up with the Joneses" but to do better than the Joneses? Why are we so driven to have more, more, more, and yes I said "we". I, too, have been a victim of the call of money. Like most people living in countries with high standards of living, I have often caught myself doing exactly what I counsel others to stop doing: working to the point of absolute exhaustion just to be able to go out and buy more "stuff." Not necessary food, not necessary shelter but just stuff that gets crammed into already overstuffed boxes, shelves, drawers and closets. Have you ever stopped in the midst of a shopping trip to actually ask yourself if you need or will use what you are shopping for? How often do you find yourself out shopping with no idea what you are going to buy, but you are certain you will know what you want when you see it.

Changing the habit of a lifetime—indeed, a habit built upon generations of western affluence will not be easy. We are constantly bombarded by the media with messages to buy things we don't need. Every year North Americans spend billions of dollars on entertainment, often with money not yet earned; the recent economic plunge was felt deepest in America because of our overreliance on credit. We are always looking for a bigger, better home or car or toys that we can't afford just to stay one step ahead of our neighbor, who has also ransomed his future earnings for a bigger, better home, car and toys.

We are fed a steady stream of media messages compelling us to work, spend, work and buy more. Though we expect to feel satisfaction from having all the things we buy, it is usually short-lived. How often have you gone out to buy something just to replace another item? The item you are seeking to replace may still work fine, it may look fine, it may have years of service left; however, it simply doesn't satisfy your needs anymore. Why? Is it possible that you only perceive that it is no longer satisfactory? All the billions in advertising spent by manufacturers and service providers would be rendered useless if we actually believed that our needs were met by this gadget or that article or treatment. To be effective, advertising must convince consumers that their needs remain unmet.

In spite of worldwide consumerism gone crazy, there are still many places in the world where money does not overshadow everything else. On a trip to Greece a few years ago I was fortunate to have an opportunity to stay with a family in a village named Finiki instead of at a hotel. In this village of less than a thousand people, I was forced to re-examine my own values. I was warmly welcomed to partake in meals which included three generations of family; everyone ate the food with pleasure and gratitude while they laughed and genuinely enjoyed each other's company. Here, among strangers, I felt a sense of family ties, tradition and community that I do not experience in my own country. I felt that they had it all: family, food, wine, love, communication and deep pride in their customs. I stayed with this family for only ten days, but when it was time for me to leave, there were lots of tears shed. I learned that the simple age-old practice of sitting, cooking and eating and talking together created a genuine human connection. I was reminded that we all need each other.

That trip made me realize that there was something missing in my own life. I vowed to try to create profound connections like those I made in that small community throughout the rest of my life. I have not forgotten that lesson. I remind myself daily of what is important to me and the values I want to live by. I resist the bombardment of media hype telling me what I need, how I should look and what I should be doing with my money. I try to step away from the madness and set my own scale of success. I love my family, respect myself, set and meet goals of self-improvement and go to sleep at night knowing that I have lived another day in accordance with my ideals.

Compulsive Behavior

Compulsive behavior, whether it is overeating, gambling, sex or substance and alcohol addiction, is based on a desire to fill an emotional need. Simply put, there is a hole inside us that has become bottomless. The more we try to fill it, the deeper, wider and darker it becomes. Compulsive shoppers have the need to buy things to get an emotional high. I think most people experience this from a purchase for a little while. But for a compulsive shopper, it is similar to the thrill and adrenaline rush of hunting or fishing for sport. The moment the hunted thing is found and conquered, the thrill begins to fade. Even on a normal scale of consumerism, people often feel buyer's remorse; after they have spent the money on something, it seems too expensive, or they realize they didn't have the money to spare. The item is just as it was when they decided they wanted it, but their perception has changed.

In the case of compulsive shopping the afflicted person often cannot enjoy the item; they may destroy it or give it to a stranger to hide the evidence of their illness. Compulsive spenders often feel guilty or out of control, signified in readings by the image of the reversed Devil. I have seen an increase in the number of compulsive shoppers who come to me for help; those who fail to look at their illness and face it squarely often end up losing everything, including their homes, their marriages, and their self respect. Like any other addiction, counseling and self-help groups are strongly recommended.

Now, on the other scale of the same compulsion is the hoarder or people who take frugality too far. I am not talking about people who can't afford things; I am talking about people whose thrift overrules common sense. When possessions are left to pile up long after their usefulness is gone they can encroach upon other aspects of your life, like mental clarity, physical space and hygiene. What is that "just in case" emergency that you have had in the back of your mind for 30 years? Sometimes you need to just get rid of the junk, either dispose of it, or, if it still can be of good use to others, give it away. When I see the tarot card representing the Page of Coins turned upside down, I ask the person if they are living with someone who is really cheap, and they usually laugh. Being cheap when you have money can be a sign of selfishness and control. Some people hoard things and money even if they don't need them, and they don't want to share. I also jokingly say, "If on your first date your new friend says 'Let's go Dutch,' run in the opposite direction!"

MAKING DO WITH LESS

I had a personal debate about including this section simply because I am not convinced that people have the desire to make do with less. We could all live with less, but not very many people are actually choosing to live with less. Making do with less is not a form of punishment even though it might feel like it. My grandmother used to say that if you wanted to know a person's priorities in life, you should look at their bank statement. Look at your own bank or credit card statement and see if your spending habits are in alignment with your priorities. What are you spending your money on? When you add up all the money spent on frivolous items and then translate that into hours worked—is it really worth it? Are you buying things that you really need, or are you buying things because you think you want them at the moment. Simplify your life and you will have less stress and more time for the things that make you happy and help keep you healthy.

If you have a financial goal such as saving for a trip or paying off a loan then think about spending money the same way you would think about cheating on a diet. If you are going to try something that is fattening or decadent, make sure it is worth those extra calories, or that extra hour at the gym. Don't jeopardize your goals for a passing lack of self-control or for convenience or just plain laziness. Before you buy something, stop and think about its usefulness and quality—don't go on a shopping binge at the dollar store just because you can! Think about the long-term effects of purchasing inexpensive but low quality items; not only is it false economy but plastic contained in the item and/or its packaging will take years to break down after disposal. Our landfills are groaning under the weight of all our plastic packaging and discarded stuff. I try to measure the stuff I buy against the experiences I could have. A year's worth of toys and cheap purchases can easily add up to the price of a family trip. I have a sign hanging in our family cottage that says, "It's not how many breaths we take that matters but the moments that take our breath away." A twist on this is: It's not the money we make that counts, but how we spend it.

Everyone has the power to choose their own relationship with money. As a psychic, I have witnessed every possible financial condition and foreseen the outcome of wealth and of poverty. I have read for paupers turned millionaires, lottery winners and gamblers on losing streaks, the greedy, the generous and the guilt-ridden. Money has risen to a status so powerful that worship is not too strong a word for the way that some people feel about having money and wanting more money. There are people willing to sell their souls, metaphorically, to get money and some who would even give up their lives to keep it. Why has money been given such power by so many? What power do you give money? What power does money give you?

MONEY AND THE FAMILY—MARRIAGE

A Polish wedding tradition calls for the wedding guests to throw coins at the bride and groom as they leave the church. The bride and groom each scramble to gather as many coins as they can with the tradition dictating that whichever one gathers the most gets to hold the purse strings throughout the marriage. It is only a tradition, but wouldn't it be wonderful if it were really that simple to sort money and power issues in a marriage?

Money and power reveal themselves in readings in a variety of ways; however, some of the symbolism is so common that it is almost universal. Following are some of the representations I see most often in readings where a spousal relationship is involved

(Though I use the term "marriage," it could refer to any sort of committed union between two people.):

When the Four of Coins makes an appearance in a reading it shows me that both parties in the marriage earn similar incomes; there is balance and a mutual underlying respect for equal financial contribution in the relationship. Talk about a perfect set-up! These couples don't experience many power struggles when it comes to who pays for what because basically, it amounts to a 50/50 split. Unfortunately, this equal and therefore beautiful partnership has shown up in only about 10% of the readings I have done.

When there is only one partner working and earning, there is a tendency toward money problems in the relationship. This will often show up in the reading as the Devil image reversed indicating control and surrounded by cards depicting coins meaning money. If children are involved and there is a designated primary caretaker who stays home there must be a realization that the stay-at-home partner is indeed working. There is tremendous responsibility that goes with looking after children and the home, if in fact these two assignments of duties are combined. It is not so in all cases. Childcare is more and more often seen as a single job, requiring all of a one adult's time and resources. Responsibilities for shopping, cooking, and care of the home may be divided between both partners.

If the partner who works outside the home does not agree that caring for children is one of the hardest jobs in the world there will be serious problems in the marriage. If there is a reluctance to give recognition over this key point, the partners should try trading off responsibilities for a week and see who has the toughest job. The efforts and contributions of both partners must be appreciated and respected or there will never be harmony in the relationship.

When I do a reading for a childless client who is solely dependent on their spouses for money I see an imbalance of power. The Devil card upside down shows that the card next to it has the control, so if it is a female card it is the female in control or if it is a male card than the male has the control. When one partner does not contribute to the household financially, a dependency relationship is created. The dynamics and dangers of a dependency relationship were discussed in chapter four, however a quick recap as far as finances are concerned is that when you are totally dependent on someone else for money, you surrender your personal power in exchange for comfort. There are some fairytale endings to these sorts of relationships, but generally, only when the financially dependent partner is engaged in some sort of meaningful work that both partners agree is significant and important, for instance, writing a book or other creative endeavor, or volunteering for charity. The bottom line is if there is a one-sided contribution but both sides want equal control in the relationship, there will be a power struggle.

I have seen cases where people with a lot of money at their disposal stay stuck in a miserable marriage because they do not want to give up the easy, lavish lifestyle to which they have become accustomed. I have witnessed situations where men and women will tolerate almost anything to maintain a life of affluence. They will submit to mental and physical cruelty, infidelity and betrayal, and humiliations of all kinds. Even if they do not involve such serious personal violations, such marriages are morally degrading;

if love had ever been in the equation, it isn't there anymore. How could love, which is based on mutual respect, possibly survive when one partner abuses their power over another? As for the partner who willingly submits to powerlessness in exchange for wealth, what happens when self-respect vanishes? Not only are you stuck in a marriage where you do not feel loved and do not feel love for your partner, you don't even love yourself. When you trade off your personal power for security you are making a very bad investment in your future.

Now what about the scenario of a money/power divide that is obvious, openly discussed and agreed upon from the very start? An example might be partners who are from opposite sides of the proverbial tracks, a real socio-economic cross-over. The old saying that love conquers all and money doesn't matter just is not so. I have seen plenty of evidence to the contrary. Here is an example of just such a romance where the woman was the one with the wealth.

One of my clients is a gentleman I'll call Brad who was born into a humble, working-class family. He worked very hard all the way through high school and won a scholarship to a good university. While there, Brad met and fell madly in love with a girl, Jennifer, from a very wealthy, high-society family—old money. Brad never felt that he was accepted by Jennifer's parents for obvious reasons; it was clear at the very first family dinner he suffered through at Jennifer's home that the two came from families, backgrounds and opportunities that were worlds apart. While Brad had worn his older brother's outworn clothes and had worked after school from an early age, Jennifer had never gone without a single thing she wanted. This difference in their attitudes toward money seemed insignificant in the early stages of their romance. However, as their relationship progressed and marriage was on the horizon, the money/power imbalance became more obvious.

Jennifer's laissez-faire attitude toward spending constantly clashed against Brad's practical, careful use of money. Jennifer's easy access to cash made Brad feel that no matter how hard he worked or how much he accomplished, he could never achieve economic equality. The feeling that he could never match the same measure of wealth that Jennifer had grown up with left Brad feeling emasculated and weak. These feelings increased as wedding plans got underway. Not only was Brad left out of the decision-making for his own wedding, he felt he could not speak up about the things that were important to him. When an obvious disparity arose between how many of his own friends and family he was allowed to invite compared with the huge guest list permitted for Jennifer's side, he was silent. How could he object when the bill was being paid by Jennifer's parents?

Each time one of these needling issues arose, Brad either rationalized it or did his best to ignore it. But ignoring the issue, as we know, does not make it go away. He began experiencing symptoms of acute stress and the closer the wedding day got, the worse his symptoms became. The more he tried to remedy his stress symptoms, the worse they got. A few months before the wedding, he became very ill and was diagnosed with colitis. Physically weak and unable to concentrate at work, Brad was passed over for a promotion that had been nearly certain only months before. He lost all self-confidence, became withdrawn and insecure, and felt incapable of living up to Jennifer's expectations.

The relationship between Brad and Jennifer had become increasingly strained; in Jennifer's view, Brad was unable to cope with the normal stress of adult responsibilities. Meanwhile, she lived at home in the lap of luxury and the money she earned was hers to spend as she wished! Not surprisingly, Jennifer broke off the engagement after deciding that Brad was simply not mature enough to enter into marriage. Poor Brad. Here was this young man wanting to please but feeling desperately insecure, very ill and totally lacking in self-confidence, and to top it all off, his wealthy fiancé dumps him!

Though it took Brad a long time to recover from the emotional and physical effects of his relationship with Jennifer, he was able to gain enough insight to understand that the relationship had been doomed to failure. Brad's feelings of insecurity had begun almost from the moment he learned of Jennifer's wealthy background. The wedding plans had been a window into how their marriage would have inevitably unfolded, with one partner holding all the power. Eventually Brad met a woman who adored and respected him for who he was, regardless of his economic status. Interestingly, this woman also came from a reasonably well-to-do family. However, having learned his lesson, Brad established equality early in the relationship, insisting that there would be no hand-outs from the in-laws and all decisions made by the couple were to be made between them alone. The last time Brad came to see me, the cards showed that his new marriage was on the right foot. His health was back to normal, his career had good potential, and he felt loved and secure. While his relationship with his wife was not without its challenges, the Four of Coins showed that money was not an issue in this union. Brad had learned to establish healthy boundaries around money and would not allow blind love or insecurity over money to compromise his feelings of personal power and self-confidence.

There are many reasons that people marry for money, and though the romance between Brad and Jennifer was not based on Brad wanting Jennifer's wealth, it certainly figured prominently in their relationship. Some people, however, marry deliberately to gain wealth and stability. The scenarios that are played out under this dynamic are vast in number, but the most frequent outcome that I witness is where the partner who accepts a lesser role in the division of power experiences a crippling loss of self-confidence. Like Brad, you are left feeling unworthy, perhaps at the beck and call of someone who you allowed to have control over you and your decisions, because after all you married for security, not love. You start to feel this person owns you—after all, they have bought and paid for everything you eat, wear, live in and play with. Doesn't sound so great when you think of it that way does it? And what about the person with the power? How does that individual feel about owning someone, just like they own the new car in the garage that will be replaced in a year by a new model? The novelty of owning a beautiful bird in a gilded cage usually wears off quickly, and the bird may find itself set free without a golden cage to live in before long.

With any lopsided power scenario where money is the motivating factor rather than love, the chances of creating a successful, happy life are slim. Whichever role you play in the relationship, you will likely find yourself feeling unfulfilled, unappreciated and anything but satisfied. Why not save yourself a lot of headache and heartache and choose the path that you know in your heart is right, before you have to learn a hard lesson? Once children are involved, the hard lessons of the adults become painful and even injurious endurance tests for the children of such unhealthy or broken marriages.

My hope is that I will see fewer and fewer marriages destroyed by the reversed Devil surrounded by coins, but the reality is most marriages are plagued by money problems. These can manifest in many different ways, some more obvious than others. I also see other money problems caused by only one partner's vice, such as an individuals' secret spending, or gambling and debt; however, these individual problems also affect and destroy partnerships. I see many people who even enter into a legal partnership, aside from marriage, unaware of their partner's genuine financial situation. Both partners will be forced to cover the debts when the business fails, or worse, the partner who was not at fault has to carry the responsibility alone since the irresponsible one has already disappeared into thin air or has no resources that creditors can seize. Either way, both partners lose.

In a marriage, which is of course a legal partnership, there is a greater danger of this happening. Pushed on by love or passion, romantic partners often choose to excuse or ignore careless spending habits and debt of their new love. But these dangerous habits will affect the credit standing of both partners after they are married. I have seen more marriages destroyed by secret spending and debt than any other issue: it comes down to trust, which once destroyed is impossible to repair. My advice is to lay it all on the table before you make the trip down the aisle. This means that all debts: credit cards, lines of credit, student loans, "pay-next-year arrangements"—everything needs to be brought out in the open before you can establish a union based on trust, loyalty and respect, all key components of love. If you have a lot of debt, you and your partner may need to get some assistance in creating a financial plan to deal with it together. Set your goals and priorities and work toward them together—and that's just how your relationship will end up.

CHILDREN

At the risk of sounding like a grumpy senior citizen, things really *were* different when I was growing up. I did not own every new toy on the market—far from it! My parents concentrated on the essentials, and play was left to the kids. As children, we had a vast wealth of the most accessible, unlimited and affordable technology known to mankind: imagination. We improvised.

It is in childhood that the imagination is formed. Do you recall the wonder of reading a book—or having it read to you—and watching all the heroes, knaves, and kingdoms come alive in your mind? Today, most kids have all that produced for them on the big movie screen, or the TV screen, or even more commonly today, a computer screen. Are we robbing our children of their imaginative childhoods by simply providing everything readymade, pre-packaged and bought and paid for? Maybe instead of buying them mountains of toys, movies and games we should devote more time to nurturing their precious, creative minds. What every kid wants most is the time and devotion of their parents. You can see this in young children all the time. All a young child craves besides the basic needs of food and shelter is to be with their mother or father, to play, to interact, to laugh, to share the stuff of imagination, and to share and soak up all the love they possibly can. Parents who incessantly throw more and more money into stuff that will keep their kids amused, or quiet, or out of sight, are sending one overriding message to their children: don't bother me. I prefer that you interact and become attached to this plastic thing, or that moving image on a screen. This kind of parenting is lazy and ineffective at best, and damaging at its worst.

As parents, we have a duty to teach our children the skills they need to get along as adults. But more importantly, perhaps, we have a responsibility to pass on the priorities and values that will help them to achieve success, happiness and a healthy self-image. Rather than bury them with mindless amusements (there is a limit even to educational toys if it means we are absent in person) we would do better to place a greater value on originality, creativity, imagination and problem-solving. And don't forget compassion, reaching out to others and willingness to explore and understand the ideas, attitudes and experiences of others. Because the modern child is inundated with media messages almost from birth, a healthy attitude toward consumerism needs to be nurtured from a very early age. Little Johnny and Sarah need to be told by adults that just because the TV shows pictures of all the latest and greatest toys, it doesn't mean that they need them to survive.

How do you control that big locomotive of consumer culture chugging at your children through the TV screen? It's easy—turn the TV off. How many households have the TV turned on 24-7 out of habit? How many times have you dropped in on a friend or neighbor for a visit, only to find yourself competing with the box that everyone is staring at, or outshouting the commercials blaring at you from the other room? Your kids can watch TV with some discretion—that is *your* job; they do not need to be inundated by the box at every moment outside of sleeping or school (and shockingly, yes, even some schools permit an overuse of television or films for discretionary entertainment. Don't kid yourself; those movies have nothing to do with education. It's about staff shortages.) You are the parent, the one in charge, you need to consider what is healthy, then set limits and stick to them. Oh sure, you will be the meanie once in awhile, but that's okay. Discipline is not a dirty word. Once you turn off that TV and get more involved with your kids, joining with then in some creative activities, you will both soon forget all about the TV. It will soon become apparent that they actually prefer to do things with you other than just sit and stare at the box that does the entertaining for them. Put together a craft box with all kinds of different supplies in it, ready to respond to the creative urge at a moment's notice. Set aside a spot in an easily accessible closet or cupboard for board games that the whole family can play and don't forget a box of dress-up clothes that will make much better use of your cast-offs than the overstuffed rag-box in the garage. If your kids are a little older, try developing an orienteering quest for them, and then get them to create one for you. There are books and websites by the hundreds or even thousands that will help you with ideas for things to do with your kids that will replace television. Of course there are all the traditional activities—music and dance lessons, art classes and organized sports, to name a few. Some of these can be cost-prohibitive, but most communities offer some sort of low-cost alternative that allows children the opportunities to experience these creative, satisfying outlets for their talents and interests. Bottom line is: some music in a church basement or a soccer ball and a square of open grass are all you really need if you have one or two committed adults to start the action.

While television is only one advertising stream that promotes consumer craziness, it is a chief source of media brainwashing aimed at children. Getting your children interested in activities that engage them physically and mentally will curb their appetite for mindless consumer babble. The beauty of engaging your child in some sort of extracurricular activity is that they will be tired, they will have had a chance to burn off some pent-up energy; they will sleep better, eat better and be all-round healthier and well-balanced individuals.

But there is one very important caution involved with creative or sports activities. Choose something your child enjoys and try enough things for them to *know* what they enjoy. Too many parents choose the activity that they feel Sally should do or excel at, usually something they did well or wished they could do but never had the opportunity to learn.

If you put Sally in piano lessons and she doesn't like them or she just is not musically inclined. then admit it and move on. At least you have given her the opportunity to try it. She may go back to it later or she may need to try a few more activities before she finds the one that really suits or inspires her. If Johnny loves to skate, then go with it, but remember you don't have to spend thousands of dollars on the best of everything right off the bat. Let him develop an appreciation first for what he is doing without all the bells and whistles. When Johnny tells you (not you telling him) and shows you (he ready and waiting at the door on time for hockey practice) that he really enjoys it, you can invest a little more. I see so many parents who are so convinced that their child is going to be the next Wayne Gretzky (usually because they wish they had been) that they go out and spend a fortune on new top of the line equipment only to find that their child would rather sit on the bench and watch (or read). Watch and listen for the clues that tell you your child is not only well-suited to an activity but actually enjoys that activity instead of throwing them—and yourself—right in at the deep end.

Teaching your children about the value and power of money is not only crucial it is every parent's duty if we are to raise a new generation of adults who are able to resist the ever-increasing tidal wave of consumerism. From an early age, you must take the time to explain to your child how money works, how bills are paid and why you need to work and earn a living. Show them how much day-to-day living costs in ways that they can understand: it requires one hour of Mommy's or Daddy's time at work to pay for the meal they are enjoying. I am in no way suggesting that you slap a plate of food down on the table with the pronouncement, "This spaghetti and meatball dinner took me two hours to pay for! So you *better* eat it!" While this illustration is a bit facetious, it's important that these sorts of lessons are done in a natural, gentle way. In this way your child will understand the importance of budgeting, saving, and thinking about choices before blinding throwing money in all directions.

You can help your child make better decisions as an adult if they understand from an early age the concept of saving up to buy what they want. Your child can save his/her allowance or gift money for the special something they want to own. You can involve your child in the process of choosing a charity for the family to *collectively* to donate to and then do it. If you are going to go shopping for a treat, set limits before you walk into the store or gift shop. Don't ever feel guilty about saying no to your child; in fact, the opposite should be true. The attitude of, "I get because I want," needs to be kept in check. If you hand out money the instant your child wants something then you can look forward a grown child who has no respect for money. Without a healthy respect for money, they will end up spending indiscriminately. They may end up broke and penniless, asking for you to bail them out on a regular basis. After all, you have always done it. The more you bail them out, the less they will respect you—and money, and they will probably never learn the basic lesson that consequences result from their own decisions. On the other hand, if you teach a child to respect money and the advantages it offers, without taking it for granted, the outcome is far more pleasant for everyone.

Wills and Inheritance

The old saying goes, "blood is thicker than water," but I have a new spin on it. My readings have shown me that money is thicker than blood. Translated, it means that blood ties are no match for greed.

When I see the images of Justice and Death combined with clubs in a reading, I know that wills and inheritance are at issue and confusion and arguments abound. Normally rational people are known to lose all reason when it comes to money and family. I often see deep, generations-old family pain and resentment surface when an inheritance or will is involved. I have witnessed siblings and cousins go tooth and nail against each other over trinkets or jewelry worth a few hundred or several thousand dollars. That piece of jewelry that Grandma left behind gets all tangled up in emotional entitlement issues like favoritism. "She would have wanted me to have it," should be engraved on a lot of tombstones. The grief that goes with losing a loved one is exacerbated by anger, resentment and a feeling of being terribly cheated. To illustrate my point, that feuding over an inheritance is folly, here are some actual cases I have witnessed of wills and inheritance tearing apart family bonds:

I had a client whose father owned a car dealership, which in turn employed her brother. When the father died the son was the executer of the will. He felt that since he worked at the dealership, he alone was entitled to the property. While the rest of the estate was divided amongst all the siblings the most valuable asset of the inheritance, the car dealership, he kept for himself. His siblings never spoke to him again.

When Vera, a family friend died, her sister went to Vera's house, ostensibly to pay her respects. While the rest of the family was occupied with other visitors, the sister rummaged through Vera's jewelry boxes to find the most valuable items. These she kept for herself. But she wasn't satisfied with that. She returned a month later with a moving van to remove all the antiques from Vera's house. Vera's children, still grappling with their loss, were not even aware of it until they began dealing with real estate agents for the sale of their mother's home. When confronted with her actions, Vera's sister was unperturbed. "After all," she reasoned, "I was her sister for longer than you were her children. She would have wanted me to have them."

A father owned a construction company and employed his three sons. One of the sons married an ambitious and controlling woman who convinced her husband to leave the family business and go into business for himself. The son obeyed his wife and went into direct competition with his father's company. The two companies continually fought over customers. Battles constantly raged, and every family occasion was clouded by this dark shadow of betrayal and conflict between the brother who left and the rest of the family. The father died of a sudden heart attack, leaving his business to the two sons who still worked for him. At the time of this writing, the son who left (with his wife pushing his buttons) is threatening to sue the other two brothers for *his* share of the family business.

I could recite stories like these for days. Money, death and family are a combination that brings out some of the most frightening and destructive behaviors ever seen amongst normally compassionate, decent people. The most damage I see is between siblings and their spouses. In the case of one of the siblings being chosen as the executor, the amount of resentment and distrust caused can be staggering. The executor of the estate is legally entitled to an executor's fee but sometimes the executor will sign off on the fee when it is a simple straightforward will. When a sibling does this, the others are usually happy. But it happens surprisingly seldom. Remember, money makes people funny. When a sibling decides to pay themselves from the estate (often too well) the anger and resentment from other siblings can cause permanent rifts in the family.

Some children calculate their parents' worth and obsess over the fact that they will inherit their wealth when their parents die; they spend half their lives thinking about how they will spend their inheritance. If there is a lot of money involved, the adult children may do very little in the way of pursuing a career, just waiting for Mommy and Daddy to pass and watch the cash roll in. This may sound vulgar to some of you, but I have done readings for many people who think this way and make no apology for it. It always surprises me just how much time and energy they put into fantasizing about their inheritance. What a sad truth it is that for many people, money means more than family, even more than having their parents with them.

Sibling rivalry is not the only peril to disbursement of an inheritance. One case that I recall involved a client's brother who suffered from early onset Alzheimer's disease. When the client's brother started to suffer from memory loss he passed all of his banking information to his new live-in girlfriend. After he died it was revealed that all the assets named in the will (stocks, savings accounts, etc.) had already been depleted. Meanwhile, the new live-in girlfriend was nowhere to be found.

While dealing with inheritance and wills may drive you and your family crazy, even worse is the case of not having prepared a will. Many people think that they are too young to have a will but the sad fact is that every day people die unexpectedly. Unfortunately, some people let the fear of facing the reality of death stop them from writing a will. Leaving a will simply protects the ones you love and ensures that they will receive any benefit from what you leave behind. It does not have to be a morbid exercise. It can actually be quite uplifting if done with the right frame of mind.

Think about what is important in your life, the people you love and how you want to be remembered. When deciding how you would like to divide your estate, size is not a factor. Even a special piece of jewelry or spoon collection might have special meaning for one person who will appreciate and cherish that gift or make the most practical use of it. A will allows you to make your wishes known and can save everyone a lot of conflict and heartache. After you have completed your will discuss it with a close friend or relative to be certain that there is no confusion about your requests and bequeaths. If you intend to donate your organs, inform your family of this decision ahead of time so that they are fully aware of this sensitive issue. Whatever manner in which you would like to be put to rest, whether it is an old-fashioned wake and burial or having your ashes scattered from a mountain top, commit it to paper, sign it and have your signature witnessed and keep it in a safe place where it can be easily retrieved.

MONEY AND BUSINESS

The way you handle money in matters related to business does not differ all that much from money and intimate relationships. When you are about to enter into a business relationship it is a lot like marriage; it is very important that all aspects of the business be discussed openly and agreed up front. Everything from who pays for office supplies to the division of labor must be covered; otherwise, on dissolution of the business, whatever the reason, ugly surprises can come up. The number one complaint that I hear in business partnerships is, "I do all the work and he gets all the money." Sound like a marriage? You bet. This is why it is so important to iron out these details right from the start, and have a written contract signed by all parties involved. This agreement can serve as protection if one partner fails to live up to his/her commitments. It also means that commitments made are clear to all parties. The black and white of the written agreement allows you to address the issue immediately before it gets out of control. Another issue is the investor/manager partnership. In this deal I see that as soon as the business makes a little money the investor steps in and cuts out the manager, leaving the manager feeling resentful. They may feel that the investor has collected the premium for all their own hard work. The need for clear roles and contractual agreements cannot be overstated. Make sure business partnerships are equitable and agreed upon before sign the paperwork or and shake hands.

When you own your own business you need to keep a clear and level head. The lines between business and personal life become so easily blurred. Some of the common issues that I have seen are: conflicts caused by differing opinions of spouses; getting too personal with staff and losing their respect; not understanding the financial standing of the business; spending too much cash without building capital; not having clearly set out goals and objectives; not knowing or understanding your market (your buyer and their motivation); and failing to commit to paper short-range and long-range business plans that identify present as well as potential new or added products, projects, services and promotions. I have experienced hills and valleys in my own businesses, and I can attest that I have learned much more from my failures; the tough lessons that emerged from my experience with the software program that Jackie and I devised (shared in chapter three) left me with a lasting sense of cautious optimism about any business venture, no matter how exciting. Enthusiasm is important, but trust, careful planning, hard work and follow-up are crucial to success.

One last word about money and business: leave money where it belongs—it's business. Money and friendship—they just don't go together. Before you agree to lend money to a friend you better decide which one you need more, the money or the friend, because if you lend the money you may never see it again, which means you may not want to see the friend again. If the friendship manages to survive for awhile, it may get bogged down by resentment, guilt, recriminations and remorse. I have seen so many people battle with their best friends or family members over lending and repaying money. The flip side of that coin is not to ask to borrow money unless you are willing to write down a terms and conditions of repayment and stick to the contract.

MEASURING SUCCESS

I once lived next door to an eighty year old man in Florida named Nick. The house that I had previously lived in was larger and more luxurious. I bemoaned this fact across the fence one day to Nick, saying that I felt that I had stepped back in life. He said that one of the most important things to learn in life was how to lower your net worth without lowering your standards. Nick lived according to his priorities. He donated to homeless organizations, regularly picked up breakfast tabs for others at the restaurant where he ate every day, and maintained his small home and garden with pride. After Nick died, I learned with much surprise that he had been a millionaire. Though he told me that he lived in balance with his bank account, he in fact lived in balance with his beliefs—a much more difficult and important yardstick. What was Nick's credo? Show charity, build community and enjoy simple pride and comfort in one's home, however humble.

Can you say the same for your own personal ideals? I know I still struggle with Nick's challenge to live simply and well.

When I first started doing readings I felt so envious of the beautiful homes that some of my wealthy clients owned. It took me a lot of self-examination and many readings to realize how true a statement is, "Money is not the best measure of success." It doesn't matter if the homes I visit are occupied by the rich or the poor— they all have dilemmas, anxieties and difficulties related to money; it is just the proportion and complexities that are different.

Perceived status and prestige aside, the real power money offers is the power of choice. With wealth comes a of wealth options; not only consumer options but also the chance and opportunity to effect change. How much change you can effect depends somewhat on the dollar value you can exercise, but pennies have been known to move mountains.

I have a few last thoughts to leave you with on the subject of finances, that most necessary and challenging aspect of modern life. Don't underestimate the power of your money to make positive changes. Vote with your dollar. Donate money to charity, work less and spend the extra time with your friends and loved ones. Instead of squandering money, lavish your time on the people and pursuits you love. Maintain a healthy respect for the power of money and be sure that you control it, instead of the other way around. Lastly, use the power of money for the higher good to change your life and our world for the better.

Chapter 7

Webs of Deception:
Affairs and
Secret Identities

Treat others the same way you want them to treat you.
Luke 6:31

The tangled web of deception: it has been cast over millions
of families, my own included. Friends and clients alike come
to me with shocking stories of lies and treachery. I have been
cheated on by both my ex-husbands. In recent years I discovered
my grandfather had secret children and relationships across the
continent, possibly all over the world. Affairs and secret identities
can destroy trust and forever alter the faith of those betrayed, and
if that faith in others is not restored, the wounds can be deep
and lasting enough to send the injured party permanently into
protection mode.

Everyone has their own dirty little secret. For most of us the things we conceal are, in the big picture, inconsequential—such as when vanity and insecurity override logic (I am thinking of my own secret stash of ridiculous weight loss products); or when desire descends, such as an undisclosed attraction—never acted upon—to your best friend's husband. But for some, secrets are carefully nurtured and built upon to create a second identity. Take, for instance, the man who is married to a woman, but is having gay relationships on the side; or the little old ladies who generate insurmountable gambling debts; and millions of people who compulsively conduct one-handed late night on-line chats in dark computer rooms worldwide. Long-term, ruinous and intentional deceit is the focus of this chapter. I will reveal the predictable outcomes of affairs and long-term deception, manifestation of deceit in the aura and tarot and incredible true accounts of secret lives.

As mentioned earlier, the tarot image of the Magician represents deception. Sometimes it is the person I am doing the reading for, or if there is a female card next to the Magician, it may mean that a woman is deceiving the person. If there is a male card next to the Magician it could mean that a man that is deceiving the client. Occasionally the Fool will also come up in readings to reveal cheaters or tricksters, but generally The Fool represents immaturity and selfishness more than any long-term betrayal. The image the Magician falls next to usually tells me what the subject is lying about. For example, a Magician next to a King or Queen represents illicit love affairs, while the Magician surrounded by coins represents secrecy surrounding money. It will be clear from the accompanying tarot images and the client's aura whether the client is on the giving or receiving end of deceit. When the Magician appears, the Hermit is usually not far behind. In traditional tarot decks, the Hermit card shows an image of an old man holding a lamp to illuminate a dark path. The Hermit indicates that the deception will be revealed; this almost always occurs within a short time after the reading.

AFFAIRS

A shocking number of my clients are either cheating on their spouse or being cheated on. There are a number of ways I can tell if a person has been unfaithful. For instance, when I see another man or a woman in the reading next to the Magician it indicates infidelity. A person's aura can show me when someone is cheating, but not in the usual way. Normally when someone is deceitful it will show as mustard yellow or olive green in their aura, but affairs don't seem to affect auras the same way as other deceptive behavior, like compulsive gambling or secret drug use. Sometimes a cheater will have redness in the center of the body, near the stomach, which normally indicates guilt, but often cheaters take a strange pride in their extramarital affairs. Usually it is not the color of an aura that reveals a cheater, but other manifestations or movements of the aura. I often do readings at parties with large groups of people. If two people present are having an affair, when they are in close proximity, their auras will reach out and touch. It's not uncommon for me to do readings for married people whose auras are connected to their secret lovers in the same room. I hate to have a front row seat to deception but sometimes witnessing the hidden energy glowing under the surface comes with the psychic territory.

Do I tell my clients if their spouses are cheating? Most people I do readings for are already aware that something is not right. My readings may serve to validate their suspicions, but I have to be discerning about how much I tell them. I have learned from experience that it is not in my best interest to flat-out say that a spouse is cheating. I rely more on statements like, "Do you have trust issues in your relationship?" Then typically the reading will reveal to me what is going on under the surface. This is a bit tricky if the person I am reading for really has no idea about the deceit. I prefer not plant the seed of doubt where none exists because I truly believe people have to learn to listen to their gut feelings and it is a very individual decision.

Before I started doing readings, my belief (drawn partly from my own painful personal experiences) was that men were unfaithful more often than women. In my experience as a psychic, I find that more women have affairs than men, but with men, cheating does not necessarily destroy the relationship. This may sound like a stereotype that reinforces outdated gender roles, but the fact is, many men who cheat have a sex-only fling while away from home and forget about it. Women, on the other hand, tend to form long-term emotional attachments. My experience from doing readings is this: affairs—long-term emotionally-invested extramarital relationships—are deceptive and undermining to a devastating degree. They usually result in one of three outcomes. While there are some variations, this story follows the pattern I have seen hundreds of times:

Arlene married Paul when she was twenty. Ten years later, she felt worn out by work and home responsibilities. After coming home from her job as an insurance agent, her second shift as mommy and housekeeper began. Cleaning, cooking, chauffeuring, and parenting—her routine had fallen into a rut. As a result, she became increasingly resentful of Paul who regularly arrived home from work after the kids were already in bed. On the weekend he became Fun Daddy. Arlene was fed up with being the responsible parent and picking up after Paul. After the kids were born, Paul had promised he would help out more. It never happened. Arlene began to hate that her voice had started sounding shrill. She felt bitter towards her husband and her family responsibilities. She and Paul became more like bickering partners in a failing business venture than husband and wife. Arlene felt an acute loss of her identity. Enter Arlene's colleague at work, Derek. They got along so well, always have interesting philosophical conversations and Derek made her laugh—something Arlene no longer shared with Paul. More importantly, she could make Derek laugh. Arlene began imagining how she might look through Derek's eyes; she like what she saw—it was her old self. The more time Arlene spent with Derek, the more alive she felt. She began to recover her sense of identity and wholeness, she felt like a person again and not a mommy or a maid. Before long the relationship became physical—Arlene fell madly in love with Derek.

Derek was married to Angela at age 26. It was very important to him to feel he was a good provider for his family, so he worked long hours and concentrated on getting ahead in his career. Investing so much of his time and energy into his work, Derek just wanted to relax when he goes home. He saw his home as a place to unwind after a long hard day; but it was such a hassle at home because it seemed that all Angela ever did was nag and make demands. Nothing he could do seemed good enough. To avoid her and her stated needs, Derek started spending even more time at the office. He enjoyed a break from all the responsibility at home. Enter Derek's colleague at work, Arlene. They got along so well, she was very attractive and she made him laugh—something his wife didn't care to do anymore. Derek could make Arlene laugh, too and he liked that. He imagined how he might look through Arlene's eyes and he liked that vision. Derek told himself this flirtation was nothing serious; it was just a fling and low-risk for complications. After all, Arlene was married too. Derek had no intention of leaving Angela for Arlene; in fact, his little fling was even rekindling his desire for his wife, whom he genuinely loved.

When the affair started, it was wonderful, surprising, exciting. Arlene felt like she did when she first began dating Paul. She hadn't felt that way in years and never thought she would again. It was so easy with Derek. She could be fun, playful and feel sexy again. Derek felt like the affair was just the distraction he needed to lighten his burden at home. He felt powerful and confident.

Suddenly, Arlene realized that she was so in love with Derek, she wanted to spend the rest of her life with him. She would leave Paul; she envisioned Derek leaving Angela and the two them starting a new life together—happily ever after! When their heads were on the pillow, Derek made wonderful promises and declarations of love. Arlene held these close to her heart, believing every word; she started to make concrete plans around their new life.

Okay, readers, you can all see what's going on here. Arlene is in love, but not with Derek; she loves a fantasy man. Derek has no intention of leaving his wife; he has far too much to lose. He's enjoying the sex and ego boost he needed. Suddenly, Arlene is talking about obligations and plans—it's time to make decisions.

The affair will result in one of the following three outcomes. Keep in mind that Arlene's and Derek's roles can be reversed in this scenario, but my experience shows that more often, the man involved ends the affair.

MODEL 1

Derek breaks off the affair and leaves Arlene heartbroken and bitter. They still have to work together making eight hours of every day unbearable for her. Paul finds out about the affair and the other sixteen hours of the day are filled with judgment and recriminations. Tears, distrust and a wall of resentment frame her marriage, which she now feels she must somehow put back together. She begs for forgiveness and regrets the affair. Paul and Arlene reconcile and recommit to each other, but once that sacred trust is broken, it is never fully recovered. While many couples do carry on after an affair the union is never the same afterwards. The post-affair marriage is comparable to a house rendered unsalable because it was a crime scene. It's the same structure but now it has a diminished value because of perceived ghosts, guilt and suspicion.

MODEL 2

Arlene leaves her husband thinking that Derek will do the same. He strings her along with promises: he will leave Angela, he just needs some time. The affair may continue for months, even years, as Arlene puts her life back together, alone, waiting for Derek to break away from his wife and family. In the meantime, Paul meets another woman and falls in love. Arlene waits on the sidelines while Derek makes up his mind. He is wracked with guilt but none of this was his fault—it was just a fling. How did Arlene suddenly make it so serious? He has no intention of leaving Angela but he doesn't want to hurt Arlene. Besides, with Arlene on her own and wanting him, the sex is better than ever. Derek knows the affair has to end and finally, he breaks it off. Arlene is left feeling humiliated, betrayed and abandoned.

MODEL 3

Arlene leaves her husband and Derek leaves his wife. They are blissfully happy until they get past the honeymoon stage. They start to have the same problems they had in their previous marriages, along with the added stress of ex-spouses and children being shuttled back and forth. The challenges of step-parenting and combining families has proved monumental. Derek begins to spend more time at work. He starts flirting with the new temp, exchanging numbers and meeting for coffee. He just needs a little break from all the problems at home, a little appreciation. I think it is obvious where this is leading. Again, not a good outcome for Arlene, Derek or, especially, the children.

Like the foregoing examples, above, most affairs I see go on between co-workers because that is where people spend the majority of their time. Almost all other affairs are with people within the same social group: friends who gather frequently, community groups or sports teams. When unhappy people are thrown together often enough, sparks can fly.

A note about your friends: be careful if you socialize with people whose loose boundaries lead to behavior that makes you uncomfortable. If you think an environment of boozy flirtation and sexual innuendo is crossing the line, make sure you make your opinion known. I have met many people who have deep regrets about crossing the line with friends' spouses. As for internet cheating, though it is reportedly widespread, only a small percentage of my clients having affairs actively sought a real-life lover through the internet or personal ads. These sorts of affairs tend to remain at a distance. Proximity equals possibility.

Any book about infidelity will tell you what the typical warning signs are: a sudden change in habits, more late nights at work, frequently being unavailable by phone. You don't have to see mustard yellow auras to know when something is up. In my opinion, the more important information is how to prevent affairs. Here is the most simple, effective method for staying connected to your partner: *make time for them.* Schedule dates in your planner and mark your calendar at the beginning of the year so the days remain reserved and sacred. Have date nights and get a babysitter or arrange for sleepovers and then reciprocate. Try to have a night alone with your spouse once a month, either away from home or at home with the kids away. You need time alone as a couple without being caught up with the pressures of everyday life, so make it a priority. If a whole night away from the kids is impossible, just take an afternoon off while the kids are at school and go for a walk, meet for lunch or coffee, or just sit on the patio with a cocktail and talk. But don't go to a movie or watch television. Do something that forces you to interact. It all sounds so simple but I'll say it again because it is more difficult to do than you might imagine: SCHEDULE TIME FOR YOUR PARTNER!

On a daily basis, talk with them. I mean really communicate, don't just serve up a laundry list of complaints or "to-dos." Check in with each other in fun ways without blaming or finger-pointing. Get your issues on the table and work them out. People tend to find it easier to tell friends or strangers how they feel rather their partner. But that's only hiding from issues. The first step to infidelity is confiding your marital problems to a third party with a vested interest, like the co-worker who flirts with you or the old flame you just reconnected with on Facebook.

There is one obvious thing missing from the above recipe for a cheat-free marriage. I have saved this ingredient till last because it is, without a doubt, the single most important component of a marriage which remains solid with open, honest communication, lasting trust and on-going commitment. That, of course, is sex. Obvious, yes, but how many marriages fall down in this area once the mortgage, kids, career and in-laws take centre stage? YOU HAVE TO HAVE SEX! It is the critical, essential bonding agent between two people. Every annoying habit, every forgotten chore, each and every burnt meal is turned to dust in the heat of regular—yes, *at least*, weekly sex. How many times is normal? Who cares?! The aggravations and differences of opinion that occur between married couples come up at least a couple of times a week—perhaps even daily. How many intimate moments of sheer physical pleasure do you need to erase those smudges? Yes, at least once a week you need to remember what it was like when you looked at your partner and wanted to tear their clothes off! If it's been years since you felt that way, it may take some time to rekindle the fire but trust me, the more often you have sex with your partner, the more often you will *want to* have sex with your partner. I know it sounds simplistic but that's because it *is* so simple. Sex is the crucial, necessary, wonderful glue that holds a marriage together. If you are bored with your partner try sprucing things up with something like Astroglide, a lubricant that is good for both of you.

If all of this sounds too much like hard work, consider the alternatives. If you do start having feelings for another person, take a good hard look at the potential loss and gain of breaking up your marriage. Consider the things you value about your partner. Consider the whys of the situation; is the other person alluring because you've been feeling old and sexually invisible lately? Are you tempted by a lover because you are in emotional distress and you have always found comfort in sex, preferably of the new and unbridled passionate variety? Are you so bored that you flirt outrageously with the neighbor just to see what will happen next? Be honest with yourself. This is the stuff you can fix without betraying the trust of the person you have promised to walk through this world with. The point is; if you can't fix it, leave. Get divorced. Betrayal is not respectful to either one of you. Intentional deceit will invoke the principles of karma, which I will discuss further in chapter 8.

SECRET IDENTITIES

Back in the schoolyard, we all learned the titillating effect of secrets. Even in adulthood, the "promise you won't tell" conversation opener creates giddy anticipation. But grown-up secrets, such as hidden sexual deviance, money compulsions, or a Jekyll and Hyde dual identity often ruin lives. Perhaps it has become more prevalent with instant accessibility to sexually stimulating material of every description available through the internet, but these behaviors exist in surprising abundance.

Secret lives, meticulously maintained and hidden, are becoming commonplace in my psychic readings.

My family had our own master of secrets, symbolized in the tarot by the Magician. My mother was raised by a foster family and not much was known about her biological family. About ten years ago, we were contacted by my cousin (my uncle's daughter) in her efforts to reunite the biological family. She had also made contact with her father's father (my grandfather) who was named Leo Bachle in his regular life. You will see in a moment why I say, "regular life."

Leo was in his 70s when my sisters and I first met him. We found him to be a sweet, charming man and we instantly adored him. He was recovering from a stroke but he still had a powerful aura. He had been married for over 40 years, and had two children from that marriage—and a lifetime of secrets.

Leo Bachle was born in Toronto, Canada. After World War II began, fifteen-year-old Leo enlisted but he was kicked out of the Army when his real age was discovered. Still inspired by the war effort, he created a comic book hero named Johnny Canuck who, from his newsprint front lines, bravely fought the Nazis. US comic strips ceased while the war was on, creating a demand for this young Canadian cartoon artist. This was the beginning of Leo's career as a famous comic book artist. He continued his Johnny Canuck stories and created new stories and characters, using names of friends and family for his characters. When the war ended, Leo moved to New York to pursue his comic book career. Multi-talented and with a gift for making the imaginary seem real, Leo also began acting and performing in nightclubs. He performed a stand-up comedy act called, "Quick on the

Draw" in which he would draw caricatures of members of the audience live on stage. Leo traveled the world with this act and met many famous people. He also entertained on cruise ships for many years under his stage name, Les Barker.

But not only did Leo have a second name, he had a second life. My cousin was not the first long lost grandchild to contact him. At the time of this writing, twelve children from eight mothers have been identified as Leo's offspring. While we don't have firm numbers yet for grandchildren and the wider net of offspring (the numbers keep increasing) we estimate it to be a much higher number, and because he travelled so much they may be all over the world. I can only imagine the shock and emotions that the two children he raised in his first family have experienced since learning of his deception. Many of Leo's lovers were abandoned, their children left behind to be raised by single mothers, or in foster homes, many experiencing their own versions of turmoil. Some of Leo's children have recently established relationships with each other. Others have decided that they don't want much to do with their newfound siblings, which given the circumstances is completely understandable.

Though Leo's legacy of secrets is vast it is not unparalleled. More and more of my clients are shocked by revelations of the people closest to them: husbands with secret sexual lives, mothers hiding the evidence of their compulsive shopping sprees, sons and daughters whose second identities would be unrecognizable to their parents. I can give a few examples:

Judy was a client of mine for about six years. She was a pharmacist in her mid-forties and had been happily married for 20 years. I had spotted the Magician image in her life since the first reading, but she always denied having any trust issues with her husband. She laughed off my insinuations of mistrust. Even though, through the years and her many readings the Magician popped up in every reading, I chose not to press the issue.

Recently Judy called me for an emergency appointment. She arrived and sat down, drawn and white-faced, in a state of disbelief. Her reading showed the Magician and this time, the Hermit was placed right above him, symbolizing a light shining on deception. I already knew what Judy was about to tell me. Judy's husband had finally revealed that he had been living a secret gay life for as long as she had known him. Finally feeling the strength to claim his true identity, he announced he was leaving her for his lover. Judy was devastated. The fact that she had never really known the man she shared her life with shook her to the core. If her marriage was an illusion, what else in her life was not real? She felt she must be losing her mind.

In situations like this, the line between psychic advisor and therapist become unavoidably blurred. As I am not a trained psychiatrist, I always recommend counseling to my clients who are experiencing deep emotional distress. Part of my work is to just provide the tissue and a safe place to land when life delivers a huge kick in the gut. Judy cringed with the shame and embarrassment of knowing that most of her adult life was built on a lie. She couldn't bear to confide in even her closest friends and so she came to me. I didn't bother to remind Judy that the Magician had been there all along; she just didn't want to believe it.

Comfort came for Judy in the knowledge that she was not alone. Hundreds of my clients have had their lives shattered by their partner revealing they are not who they claim to be. While this example has homosexuality at the root of the deception, it is most certainly not always the case. The issue is not about a negative value judgment on the homosexual or any other sexual or lifestyle choice, but rather about the risks and pain caused by not being true to yourself and those you love. Deception and betrayal are the weapons of greatest injury and are so often used by people who have no intention of hurting others. Sometimes it takes a lot of courage and honesty to get your head and heart in alignment, but living authentically is always worth it.

Financial deception is another way deceit manifests. A client and friend has an ugly little shop-at-home habit which she tries to conceal from her husband. She hides the bank statement as soon as it come and has her secret purchases delivered to other addresses; she will even give away the brand new items without ever opening the packaging. In spite of my urging to seek counseling, she continues on this course. She is in danger of losing her home, her husband and her family's trust and respect, yet she continues to rush headlong down the "Buy Now!" route to ruin.

Shopping addictions, while sneaky and harmful, are usually motivated by a deeper psychological need and judging by my readings, they can't really be painted with the same brush as other deceptions. The tarot usually shows this kind of activity as the Devil upside-down with adjacent coins, which always denotes a loss of control around money. Compulsive gamblers, from card sharks to bingo grannies, will show the reversed Devil as well.

Long-term, intentional deceit is the most destructive weapon ever wielded against a relationship: it bludgeons to death the gift of trust. While the scale of deception is vast, the outcome of it is as simple as this: the pain you release into the world will always return.

Some of my most painful life lessons, both in my career and personal life, have been delivered at the hands of Magicians. At times I have retreated back into my shell with disappointment. This much is certain: you cannot let the trials in life keep you down forever. We all need to hide and lick our wounds from time to time, but learn your lessons and move on. If you remain in your shell, you will go through your life untouched and without meaning. Listen to the song from Chumbawamba that says, *I get knocked down, but I get up again, 'cause you're never going to keep me down.*

Eight

The Wheel of Life

I again saw under the sun that the race is not to the swift
and the battle is not to the warriors and neither is bread to the
wise nor wealth to the discerning nor favor to men of ability.
For time and chance overtake them all.

Ecclesiastes 9:11

The significance of the tarot deck and the insights it can
provide are based on the belief that the images in the cards reveal
what is going on inside the mind and life of the subject. The tarot
shows you what is going on behind the scenes in your life and
can describe your internal dialogue. What you feel inside will
always be manifested in life; your interior world of beliefs, fears,
hopes and dreams is reflected in what goes on in your day-to-day
life. This also applies in reverse: if you are trying to understand
problems in your life you only need to examine you own thoughts,
beliefs, prejudices, fears and motivations to make sense of any
circumstance you are experiencing.

This is good news because it means that you hold the power and therefore you have options. Since you choose what thoughts are in your head, what words come out of your mouth and what you feelings you hold in your heart, you have the power to change any situation for better or for worse. The choices we make every day direct the course of our lives. Remember the power behind the split path reading. Alternate destinies will unfold based on your conscious decision. Choosing the responsible path doesn't mean that you will always have a smooth or easy road to walk but you will be putting your energy and strength into a choice that is in keeping with your higher consciousness.

In the imagery of the tarot, the Wheel of Fortune is traditionally interpreted as the eternal wheel of life; some people say it represents destiny and inevitability, others say it means that a sudden turn of fate is about to play a major role in the life of an individual. When the Wheel of Fortune appears in a reading it may mean that there are forces at work behind the scenes that will alter the client's life in ways they cannot imagine. But it also may signify a time when one must recognize that there are things happening outside of one's life that are not within one's control. If you find yourself in the grip of forces, circumstances and decisions outside your control, your best course of action is to simply accept it and go with the movement of the wheel.

There are many things that we cannot control: the world economy, aggression, injustice and poverty, to name a few. What you can control are your actions in the here and now: your thoughts, your actions and your decisions will determine what will come next. Your willingness to take responsibility for the outcome of your choices can make the difference between a life lived with intention and one in which you feel powerless.

We touched briefly on the concept of karma in chapter one. Simply put, karma is a spiritual concept that explains cause and effect. Think of it as the spiritual equivalent of Newton's rule of physics: For every action there is an equal and opposite reaction. Karma is often mistakenly viewed as punishment or retribution but it is in fact a logical outcome for our thoughts and deeds. There are consequences for everything we do and say—this is simply how energy works. When people consciously inflict pain and misery on others, they release a wave of negative energy (or bad karma) out into the universe and like a boomerang, that negativity will find its way back to its origins, often picking up more negative energy on the way. You may have heard of the principle of the three-fold wish: if you wish harm on someone and you send that wish out into the universe, it will come back on you with three times the intensity.

Here in the west the word karma is usually used to reference the axiom that one reaps what one sows in this lifetime. In cultures that believe in reincarnation, karma extends beyond this life and into previous and future lives. Karma and the abuse of energy are not to be taken lightly.

It is very important for us to understand that energy is also constantly interchanging, attracting other energy to itself and moving away from energy that is not consistent with itself. Simply put, this is the principle of "like attracts like." Whatever we put out will always come back.

There is a lot of talk lately about random acts of kindness; it is a concept that is starting to take hold in our world of abundance and having everything we need. More and more people are discovering the power behind small, seemingly insignificant charitable acts. It's like the proverbial drop of water—by itself it doesn't amount to much. But added in with thousands or millions of other drops of water it can sustain life. If each and every one of us performed one act of kindness every week, we could see the world transform before our very eyes.

CHANGE AND LOSS

To compare life to a wheel, we see that it is always turning, always changing like the changing of the seasons or movement of the tides. Because of this constant movement of the wheel of life we pass through cycles of highs and lows; but if we are going through a time of challenge, difficulty or suffering we can take comfort in knowing that as the wheel of life turns, so will our circumstances. Winter gives way to spring; summer cannot last forever but as it passes away, our lives flood with the vibrancy of autumn until we find ourselves moving into the quiet, restful time of winter again. Life also has its seasons including anticipation, joy, struggle, loss and restoration.

Though many people welcome change and adjust to it with enthusiasm, it is a natural inclination for humans to resist change. Change means loss and even if the loss is of something that is no good for you, such as outdated attitudes or unhealthy perspectives, the prospect of change is sometimes so threatening that people forget that what they cling to is no longer useful or is actually harmful.

Buddhists have a name for the constant cycle of life and birth, which is *samsara*. Other religions embrace teachings that all of life follows a continuum of constant change, a never-ending spiral where humans learn about truth through repeated experiences of life, death and rebirth. Images of spirals and wheels predominate in many ancient religions and can be seen in the work of many spiritually inspired artists. The idea of a never-ending wheel of life can be a source of comfort and hope rather than cause for fear of change or loss of control.

If you live in sync with the laws of the universe, every choice you make in life is the right choice for the lessons you need at the time. Just as we learn in the ways that we deal with change and loss, we also learn by the paths we choose and the results we achieve by following our choices and seeing our decisions through to their natural conclusion. A task or commitment left incomplete interrupts the natural flow of energy. If the Wheel of Fortune appears in a reading, it may be a reminder to keep the commitments or promises you have made in order to keep energy flowing through your life in a healthy way.

If you live your life with good intention and a positive attitude, if you help people and share in responsibility for protecting the resources of the earth, then you are making good choices that will have a far-reaching effect. If you truly do the best you can do with everything you have, then good things will come to you.

ENERGY AND GRIEF

There are different realms of energy, some within our own aura and some far beyond our realm of existence. Since approximately 70 percent of the human body consists of fluids, we are all excellent conductors of energy. Albert Einstein proved that energy can never be created or destroyed. So when our conductor of energy, our body, dies, the energy that is released is transformed. In other words, I believe that when we lose a loved one we lose their physical presence but their soul still exists and the love that we shared never dies.

Whether or not you believe in an afterlife, death and loss are an unavoidable part of the human journey. Finding peace in loss does not require you to believe in angels or to subscribe to a particular faith, but reaching a state of acceptance and acknowledgement of loss requires a psychological healing process that takes courage, self-honesty and above all time. There is little that can be of comfort in the first days, weeks and months following the loss of a loved one. This is what I call "ground zero." It is a time to respect your feelings and not simply push them away or deny that you are in pain. Let other people carry the load for awhile. While there are always important things that must be taken care of, making yourself insanely busy immediately following the loss of a loved one will not make the hurt feelings disappear; they may hide out for awhile behind your busyness, but they will be waiting for you as soon as the ink dries on the last details. Be gentle with your feelings in the early stages of your grief. When you feel ready, look for ways to find comfort and meaning in your loss.

Grief has not been stranger to me and comfort in my own sorrow has sometimes come in unexpected ways. When my son Carson was ten months old, he was playing in his crib one day. Suddenly, he said the name "Cole" as clear as could be; this was an affirmation of my own belief that my son who died shortly after birth was a guardian angel watching over Carson. While that story may not strike a chord with your beliefs, it held special meaning for me. However you find peace in loss, it will be unique to your needs. If you have a strong religious faith, the community of your place of worship may bring you comfort. If you are not religious, then family and friends or a support network may help you. For some people, therapy may be of great benefit in helping to sort out the complexities of thoughts, questions and emotions that arise when facing the truth of mortality. Whatever way you choose to grieve, bear in mind that the energy of the love you shared lives on and should be acknowledged. Many people find peace by honoring the memory of their loved ones by planting a tree, commemorating a public facility, or by making a donation to a charity.

Many of my clients feel they are facing life's challenges alone, but my work has taught me otherwise: our struggles are more similar than they are different. People often think that psychics should be able to see their own futures and know things, such as winning lottery numbers—I wish! Unfortunately, it just doesn't work that way. I can claim a fair share of my own poor choices, failures and problems. Many of my lessons have been painful, but I see them now as stones in my path that helped me to develop and discover my true calling. I write from a place of empathy, sharing lessons of joy and pain that can help to shed light on everyone's path. Hopefully this book will cast some light on your own issues and provide answers that will guide you to a better path leading to a more positive experience of life.

Appendix

CLEARING THE AURA

I recommend the following stones and crystals for improving the energy of your aura:

Hematite helps in grounding the aura and improves mental and emotional clarity.

Copper assists the flow of energy, especially helpful if you feel stuck in your life; also helps improve blood circulation and arthritis.

Citrine helps you to attune to your higher self, or to connect emotionally and spiritually with deceased loved ones or your guardian angels.

Clear Crystal Quartz helps to absorb negative energy.

Rose Quartz can help in attracting your soul mate into your life, or if you are already in a relationship, it can help restore romance and soothe disagreements.

Jade has been used for centuries to improve energy around money; it can help you to take control of your finances, or attract money.

Topaz helps to heal the body and soul.

Make sure that when you are using stones for their beneficial properties, they are somewhere within your auric field. Wear them as jewelry or carry them in your pocket, close to your body.

Before and after use, stones should be put in a container and covered with dry sea salt or sea salt dissolved in water and allowed to sit overnight to cleanse any negative energy.

SMUDGING

I use white sage to cleanse the aura. I place it in an ashtray or in a fireproof dish and light it up, then almost immediately blow it out so that it begins to smoke. Then, with my hand, or as in Native practice, with a feather, I wave the smoke over the top of my head and around my body. If you want to cleanse negative energy from a room in your house or your place of work, wave the smoke around all the windows, doors and mirrors and as you do so say, "I release all negative energy from this home (office)."

Write a letter to the Universe, God or your Higher Power

I know this sounds silly but when you write down what you really want in life and release the message to a power higher than yourself, you acknowledge surrender and acceptance to the best outcome. This gives you peace of mind. This practice works better if the letter is mailed at the time of a full moon.

Making lists and checking twice, three times or more

When you write things down they become clearer in your mind. Write down the good qualities about yourself and all the people, things and circumstances that make your life better. Whenever you have negative thoughts or feedback, you will have a ready list to remind you of all the good things in your life.

Replacing Negative Files (From Chapter Two)

Part 1

Make a list of all the positives in your life. Don't forget to include the many things you probably take for granted: all your senses and faculties, your mobility, intelligence, etc. Keep this list where it will be near at hand when you are just waking up in the morning.

(Another tip to "fast-track" your re-conditioning regime: Read this list just before you go to sleep at night. These positive thoughts will replay while you sleep. You will be surprised at how quickly your psyche begins to absorb these new messages.)

Part 2

Do this exercise just as you are waking up, before your mind is seized by your habitual negative thoughts.

Visualize your life in the present moment as a filing cabinet. Open the filing cabinet and retrieve a file containing a negative thought. For instance: "As a small child, every day I cried after my mother left me with a babysitter to go to work. If my mother had not chosen a career over staying at home to look after me as a child, I would not be suffering from the overwhelming fear that my spouse will leave me one day."

Now, replace that negative message with a positive one. For instance: "As a small child, every day I cried after my mother left me with a babysitter to go to work. This experience left me with a deep certainty that one day I would be left to care for myself entirely on my own. I now see this experience as a life lesson. Because I had a deep unconscious belief that I would have to look after myself, I have mastered many skills. I have developed an independent personality and confidence that comes from knowing that I am capable of taking care of myself."

Positive affirmations

Support your work in replacing your negative "files" with these positive reinforcements:

- I recognize and accept the fact that I cannot change the past.
- I recognize and embrace the truth that only I have the power to change my perception of the past.
- I choose to change my future by changing my perception of the past.

(Add more of your own)

Kim Sartor

A lifelong psychic, Kim has been performing professional psychic readings for ten years, gathering a loyal following of regular clients, some of whom have provided testimonials included on page 196.

She is also an entrepreneur whose products have been showcased on the Donnie and Marie Show, Canada AM, The Early Show with Bryant Gumbel, and MacLean's magazine as well as newspapers and radio programs across the continent. Kim has even given an on-air live reading for Liza Fromer, former co-host of Breakfast Television, with amazing results. She has also provided her services for many charity events across Canada.

Kim can be contacted through:

www.kimsartor.com

info@kimsartor.com

"Energy tells your story. The more you focus on your beliefs, problems or desires, the more those thoughts become reality. Be careful of the thoughts you hold onto, because they become part of you. Auras show me the results in Technicolor."

Client Testimonials

I remember when I went to see Kim just after my father's death and she told me things that I could not even fathom, all of which occurred exactly as she predicted. Do you believe in psychics? I would say that you need to keep an open mind. Some people really do have the gift of sight, and Kim is one of them—a real psychic. I trust Kim. She has the ability to see and, more importantly, decipher what she sees in the tarot blocks. All I can say is that I applaud the day that I met Kim; she has opened my eyes to the past, the present and the future.

Catarina Flack, Freelance Writer

I first met Kim in the summer of 2006. In the time that I've known Kim, I've had about six or seven readings, all of them extremely accurate. Kim has told me things about myself and my life that I've never told anybody. For example, about a month after my grandfather passed away I went to see Kim. I didn't mention anything about my grandfather's passing. As soon as I sat down she said, "You've got somebody with you. I can feel him in the room. Did somebody close to you die very recently?" She didn't know me or anyone that knew me, and I hadn't even opened my mouth yet. There was no way she could have known how close I was to my grandfather, and that I was grieving his passing.

Heidi Pokorny, Manager, Sponsorship, Events and Promotions

I have found Kim's readings so spot-on it's almost unbelievable. She begins by reading the past . . . couldn't have been more accurate about my previous marriage and personal relationships if I had told you the stories myself. She pegged personalities to a tee and described my experiences as if she felt them herself. . . . She told me of my father's health issues, cause of death and even referred to him by name. She also described a few situations I was going through at the time . . . and indicated the people and personalities involved, and even told me the outcome. She was dead-on. Whether she spoke of the past or the present she was accurate, and some of the things predicted for the future have already come to pass. I believe it is just a matter of time before all comes to pass, or perhaps I will change my destiny now after making choices as a result of having a heads-up from Kim.

Madeline Mount, Health Care Provider / Business Owner